Safe Haven
MARRIAGE

Safe Haven
MARRIAGE

A Marriage You Can Come Home To

DR. ARCHIBALD D. HART
DR. SHARON HART MORRIS

W PUBLISHING GROUP
A Division of Thomas Nelson Publishers
Since 1798

www.wpublishinggroup.com

SAFE HAVEN MARRIAGE

Copyright © 2003 Archibald D. Hart and Sharon Hart Morris.

To protect the privacy of individuals, each story is a summary of typical aspects of numerous couples.

Published by W Publishing Group, a division of Thomas Nelson, Inc., P.O. Box 141000, Nashville, Tennessee 37214.

Scripture quotations used in this book are taken from The Holy Bible, New International Version, copyright © 1973, 1978, 1984 by International Bible Society. Used by permission of Zondervan Publishing House.

Library of Congress Cataloging-in-Publication Data

Hart, Archibald D.
Safe haven marriage / by Dr. Archibald D. Hart and Dr. Sharon Hart
Morris.
    p. cm.
ISBN 0-7852-8947-X
1. Marital psychotherapy—Popular works. 2. Marriage—Psychological aspects—Popular works. 3. Emotions. 4. Attachment behavior. I. Morris, Sharon Hart. II. Title.

RC488.5.H375 2003
    616.89'156—dc21   2002154343

Printed in the United States of America
03 04 05 06 BVG 9 8 7 6 5 4 3 2 1

Thank you, Mike, for your love and support over the years.

To my sons, Vincent and Alan, precious to my heart—
you both light up my life.

Thanks, Dad, Mom, Catherine, and Sylvia,
for encouraging me and always being there.

—SHM

To the precious gem of my heart—my safe haven partner and
encourager, Kathleen—and my three daughters: Catherine, Sharon,
and Sylvia, who together are the most precious persons in my life.

—ADH

CONTENTS

ACKNOWLEDGMENTS

Thank you to Brent Bradley for introducing me to emotionally focused therapy and to Susan Johnson for her training and continued support. Your influence has impacted my work and my own relationships. I thank my colleagues and supervisors at La Vie Counseling Center, who are a constant source of support. To the couples who have taught me by trial and error how to foster a safe haven marriage—your vulnerability is humbling.

Thanks also to Ernie Owen, Laura Kendall, and W Publishing Group for their belief in us and in this book; and to Lela Gilbert for her skillful editing. To all our friends, colleagues, and loved ones, thank you for all your patience, encouragement, and prayers. Thank you, Mike May, for your love. Without each of your contributions, this book would not have been possible. We thank you for sharing your lives so that other lives can be touched.

—Sharon Hart Morris

INTRODUCTION

*A*re you emotionally connected with your husband or your wife? Do you sense that your spouse understands and values you? Is your wife or your husband a safe haven—a trustworthy person with whom you can be completely secure, knowing that you are loved, accepted for who you are, and cared for above anyone else? Do you feel you can trust your spouse with the deepest parts of your heart?

While some of you can answer these questions with a resounding "yes" or even "most of the time," many marriage partners cannot. Even if they are committed to a lifelong marriage, for a variety of reasons they feel to some degree emotionally disconnected from their spouse.

Maybe your heart sank as you read the first paragraph of this introduction, and you wondered whether such a relationship was even possible for you. You may fear that your spouse is not capable of changing enough to make such a marriage possible. Or perhaps you don't know if you can risk being vulnerable so to become a safe haven to your spouse.

We've written this book for you, and for all those who long to be emotionally connected with their spouse. Whether you are in a stable marriage that simply needs some strengthening, or in a painful and empty marriage that is almost on the rocks, we believe that we have something to offer you, something that is distinctively different from what you may have found in other marriage handbooks.

We call the type of marriage we are proposing here a safe haven marriage, and our choice of terms is very intentional.

We are not calling it a "happy" marriage or a "romantic" marriage; we are aiming to help you create a "safe haven" marriage. And when your marriage is a safe haven, happiness and romance will naturally ensue. If your marriage is not very happy or satisfying, chances are it is not an emotionally safe place for either you or your spouse.

During the process of working toward a safe haven marriage, we will not focus on instructing you to become a better communicator or to take your spouse out on more dates. These may be important, but our focus is going to be on *developing an emotional connection.* If you don't have a good emotional connection, increased talking or frequent dates will merely end in more conflict. Only when your emotional connection is secure do talking and dating become genuinely exciting and satisfying.

This book will help you and your spouse understand your relationship in a new way, exploring and examining your marriage through a lens called *attachment theory.* Our method of doing marital therapy is based on this theory, and it is called *emotionally focused therapy.* Much of what we share here is based on these approaches. This book is intended for couples who are seeking help, although we hope that counselors will find our work beneficial as well.

The chapters provide step-by-step methods for emotionally connecting, healing past hurts, and fostering a closer attachment bond between spouses. And what could be more important? Our culture reflects a tragically high divorce rate—more than 50 percent. This statistic tells us that couples are unable to maintain a relationship for the long haul. And it also makes us aware that counselors are not successfully impacting struggling couples in their plight. Perhaps we're beginning to understand why.

For years, marital therapy has focused on communication skills and resolving conflicts. Andrew Christensen and the late Neil Jacobson spearheaded the behavioral approach to marital counseling, and both spent decades of their lives researching, only to come to recognize the limitations in their widely used and accepted counseling methods. They reported, "A good third of couples did not respond to the treatment, and even among those who did respond positively, a substantial number relapsed in the years following treatment. From a scientific standpoint, the best available wasn't that good."[1]

Why have the behavioral and many other approaches been so unsuccessful? Because, in order to perform the tasks necessary to make the therapy effective, couples need to be emotionally connected. Conflict resolution and communication skills don't pump life back into an ailing marriage, and they don't help couples trust each other. These techniques are helpful, but they don't enable couples to feel safe, loved, valued, and understood.

In fact, some couples learned to use their newfound communication skills to fight more effectively. Consequently, when their attempts to repair their relationship failed, they were left feeling more emotionally disconnected, unloved, and unvalued than ever. They became hopeless, coming to believe that the problem in their marriage was not that they were unable to emotionally reconnect, but that they had simply married the wrong person. Many live in a lonely marriage while others choose divorce.

Our marital counseling field has long awaited a change, a fresh perspective on marriage that can truly make a difference in the way couples walk through life together. We believe that the attachment theory provides that much-needed change.

As counselors, we need to be fostering acceptance, not skills. We should be teaching couples to talk about their feelings, rather than teaching them new techniques. We need to help couples heal their hearts so they can draw closer to one another, rather than guiding them through another six steps or five keys or seven principles. *Rather than individuating, skill building, and problem solving, couples need to feel emotionally safe, close, cherished, and respected. Only then can they intertwine their hearts and souls and become one, as God intended.*

We think there is such an approach sweeping through our field: emotionally focused therapy. Emotionally focused therapy was conceptualized in the mid-1980s by Susan Johnson and Les Greenberg, two Canadians who watched their clients and allowed the changes they saw in these couples determine how they could best be helped.

Johnson and Greenberg found that the attachment bond of a couple was, above all else, most crucial to the longevity of their relationship. They discovered that if a couple fostered a close and secure attachment bond, they were better able to problem-solve on their own, utilizing the skills and techniques they possessed naturally or were taught through enrichment. On the other hand, if a couple could not emotionally connect, they simply would not have a healthy or long-lasting marriage. It is because of this reality—*emotional connection must precede all other skills, techniques, and methods in marital therapy*—that we have written this book.

In case you are wondering, we, the authors, are a father/daughter team. I (Arch) am a clinical psychologist who has worked with many couples in marital therapy. But Sharon, who has a Ph.D. in marriage and family therapy, is the real expert. The approach we are recommending comes directly from Sharon's experience with emotionally focused therapy and her research with couples.

How should you put this book to work in your relationship? Ideally, you will read it as a couple and, every now and then, discuss how the book affects each of you. Try to set aside times when you can discuss how the process is affecting you or to become aware of issues it raises in your relationship. If your partner refuses to participate in any way, then read the book for yourself. As you read, we encourage you to open your heart to God and allow Him to provide His wisdom, strength, and blessing on your efforts. With His help, this could be the beginning of the best years of your life together.

However, some men and women are so injured by childhood neglect, abuse, or trauma that they find it difficult, perhaps even impossible, to take emotional risks or to express their feelings openly and honestly as we suggest in the following chapters. If you and/or your spouse find this to be the case, we strongly advise you to seek professional help—a Christian counselor, pastor, or other qualified therapist to assist you as you seek the healing you need. This is even more important if you are dealing with abuse, violence, or threats to yourself or your children. If that is your situation, please get professional help immediately.

It is our sincerest prayer that as you read this book, by yourself or with your spouse, through God's grace you will both be changed and will experience each other in new and nurturing ways. We also encourage you to continue your journey of fostering a close connection with your spouse beyond the pages of this book.

Wherever you are on your marital journey, we pray that you and your spouse will form a strong and lasting emotional connection. And as you are bonded into one, secure enough to share the secrets of your innermost hearts, we know your marriage will become the safe haven for which every couple yearns and hopes and prays.

—Archibald D. Hart, Ph.D.
Sharon Hart Morris, Ph.D.

Part One

UNDERSTANDING
ATTACHMENTS IN MARRIAGE

Chapter 1

A SAFE HAVEN FOR YOUR HEARTS

Safe haven. n. A trustworthy person to whom you can turn, knowing that person will be emotionally available and will respond to you in a caring manner.

The harbor was straight ahead, a welcome sight. All day the wind had blown in our faces as waves crashed against the side of the boat. The sun burned hot on our shoulders. Sailing the waves of the Pacific Ocean on Dad's twenty-eight-foot sailboat had been exhilarating but exhausting. In fact, at times it had even been a bit scary because the sea was rough and the Santa Ana winds were strong. Now that we were on our way back, nothing could have been more comforting and soothing than the sight of the harbor entrance. We gratefully approached the peninsulas of large rocks that reached out and around us, marking the entrance to the safe haven.

My dad—who is the coauthor of this book—reminded us, "Red buoy has to be on the right when returning," as every sailor is supposed to know. When we crossed the harbor entrance, the waters suddenly became calm, even peaceful. It reminded me of the time when Jesus spoke to the storm and commanded it to be still. The harbor really was a place of safety, where all peril was behind us.

A SAFE HAVEN

This image of a safe haven, a place that protects us from the raging seas of life, is central to what we want to share in this book. It is a metaphor for what every marriage should become. All couples, when they marry, look forward to seeing their relationship become a haven for their hearts. As counselors, we call a marriage that is a refuge from the pressures and problems of the outside world a "safe haven" marriage.

Marital partners yearn for their spouse to see them for who they are and to be there for them. Spouses want to be fully understood, accepted, and valued by their mates. We're sure you feel that way too. And even though you and your spouse may be very different, each of you having your own dreams, ideas, expectations, and needs, both of you surely share the desire for your relationship to be a place where you can safely return for comfort and loving reassurance—a safe haven.

Unfortunately, marriage doesn't always turn out to be a place of safety. It can become a battleground where emotional safety is demolished by hot emotions and negative ways of interacting. It can become a stormy, emotionally unsafe place. To illustrate why the approach we are taking is so important and to lay the foundation for what is to follow, let's take a brief look at what an unsafe marriage can be like.

WALKING ON EGGSHELLS

Meet Jack and Adelle Carpenter, who are sitting in a counseling office. They have been married for six years and have two small children. Adelle became pregnant on their honeymoon, so as a husband and wife, they never really had time to build and grow their marital bond, which takes about two years. Nowadays, their life together is a whirlwind of working, caring for two children, and trying to save enough money to buy a house.

Fighting usually begins at the Carpenters' when Adelle feels that Jack has not helped around the house the way she'd like him to. She usually tries to talk to him about her concerns. "Of course I'm aware of the importance of communication," she says. But Adelle feels that Jack is never available for important conversations. "And when we do manage to talk," she reports, "I have to drag out of him how he feels." She experiences her husband as being both aloof and uncaring. "He's a good father, but he's not the least bit helpful," she concludes.

Meanwhile, Jack has a somewhat different view. He says that they argue because, "Adelle is always unhappy with me. It's either that I haven't done what she wanted, I've said something hurtful, or I've done something wrong with the kids."

Jack goes on to say, "I walk on eggshells most of the time with Adelle. No matter what I do, it just isn't good enough. I say something that upsets her, or I forget to do something she thinks is important. Then I get it. She yells, criticizes, and makes me feel like a failure as a husband. No matter what I do, I can't convince her that I really do care for her. Quite frankly, I'm tired of the whole thing. I've pretty much shut down."

Adelle's response? "He just doesn't take care of responsibilities, so I have to keep reminding him. If I don't remind him, nothing will ever get done. I have to work really hard at getting him to share himself with me. It is so draining that it's unbelievable. I feel completely alone in this marriage."

A NOT-SO-WELL-BLENDED FAMILY

Next, meet Kevin and Anne Preston, who have been married for fifteen years. Anne has a son from her first marriage. Kevin has a twenty-five-year-old daughter from his first marriage, and together they have two-, eight-, and ten-year-old daughters. Kevin and Anne learned early in their marriage that there are some subjects they simply shouldn't discuss with each other. When they do, a fight invariably explodes, and their fights leave them angry for days.

Most of the Prestons' hot topics involve their children. Kevin generally tries to avoid such discussions. Anne ignores his reticence and brings them up anyway, with great intensity. Kevin's avoidance of discussions about their children has always made Anne feel alone; she long ago concluded that Kevin doesn't care as much for her as he does for his daughter. By now the hot topics have expanded—even the smallest things are able to ignite big arguments that send Anne and Kevin into a spin cycle. Unfortunately, both of them are too preoccupied with getting their point across to hear what the other is actually trying to say.

Anne complains, "I learned early on not to come between Kevin and his daughter. I feel he defends her and makes me the evil stepmother. He tells me I'm too emotional. Maybe I am, but I long for him to understand how I feel. He tells me I'm panicking. 'Just calm down!' he says. Then he walks away. I call up my sister and talk, but I long to be able to talk to him."

Kevin describes his experience. "She just doesn't trust me. She always finds something wrong with the way I do things. And yes, I back off. Of course I do! I don't want to fight. So I avoid these discussions and walk away. I guess you could say that I tune her out, but otherwise we get into overheated fights that go nowhere."

Not a Safe Haven

Another husband who participated in our research described his marriage this way: "I simply don't feel emotionally connected with my wife. Our relationship is not a safe place for my heart. Don't get me wrong—I love my wife very much. But I just can't turn to her and trust her with my innermost feelings. I have tried over the years, but it always ends up with us fighting. We each defend our point of view, and we are both left frustrated. I don't feel seen or understood. That's okay. I protect my heart, keep things to myself, and keep busy. I also pray a lot, and that gets me through."

Tragically, this man's wife wrote an almost identical response when she turned in her research questionnaire. And this mirror of mistrust highlights the saddest aspect of this whole problem: Invariably, both partners in a marriage have exactly the same desire for emotionally safe connectedness. They simply blame one another for not having a safe haven, while having no idea how to achieve it. Instead, they are locked in a vicious cycle of arguing. This pattern keeps their disappointments, hurts, and anger at the surface of their marriage and buries their hearts beneath a mountain of defenses.

How Safe Is Your Marriage?

Do some of these conversations sound all too familiar to you? Do you feel strangely alone, even though you've been married for years? Are the ways you try to get your spouse to understand you doing more damage to your marriage than good?

Reflect for a moment on the last few times you and your spouse had a quarrel. What typically sparks your disagreements? You probably see things differently. Perhaps your spouse has a habit of making hurtful remarks whenever you try to tell him how you feel about something. One of you tries to make a point. The other says, "Why are you always so critical?" and gets defensive. And the more your spouse defends himself, the more you try to explain what's wrong.

Perhaps you find yourself in a marriage where each of you tries very hard to get the other to understand your perspective, even though the harder you try the more contentious it all becomes. Before you know it, you are stuck in an emotional whirlwind that keeps driving you apart, leaving both of you feeling misunderstood and unvalued. Sometimes you are able to navigate your way through such an argument and come to a mutually acceptable understanding, but that may have begun to happen less and less often. You both cling to your side of the story. Your voices get louder. Eventually someone retreats into a distant corner of the house.

In the aftermath, it could be days before civility and comfortable conversation return. You sweep your hurts under the rug, the place where all your unresolved hurts figuratively end. Getting back together after such a storm is always difficult in an unsafe marriage.

Can you envision a marriage in which you would feel safe enough to say what you feel? In which you were assured that your spouse would respect, or at least attempt to understand, your point of view? Under those circumstances, at the end of an argument you could come back together and reestablish your emotional warmth. You would be able to say to each other, "I don't want to hurt you, and I know you don't want to hurt me. We are both trying so desperately to feel understood. I don't think we did a good job of it. Maybe we can start over. This time I'll make a special effort to listen as best I can to your point of view. Will you do the same for me?"

Often, it is precisely because couples love each other so much that strong, negative emotional gales arise, stirring up giant waves of anger, hurt, and disconnection. Each fear-provoking encounter is like another breaker against the hull in a storm-tossed ocean. Naturally you feel edgier, more fearful. After enough of these storms, you become overly cautious of every encounter with your partner. Marriage becomes an unrelenting, tumultuous voyage with no sign of a safe harbor anywhere in sight.

DISCOVERING YOUR SAFE HAVEN

How to discover and develop a safe haven in your own marriage is the focus of this book. We have a heartfelt desire to help couples like you discover emotional safety in each other. And besides seeing your pain alleviated and your hearts comforted, we also know that this is God's heart cry for all marriages. The many students, counselors, pastors, and couples whom we have taught and counseled using the safe haven approach have confirmed that it is the cry of their hearts as well.

Just like Tom and Yvonne Richards.

"I just want you not to be mad at me all the time." Tears rolled down Yvonne's cheeks as Tom, his voice softened with sincerity, spoke these words to her. They had been married for twelve years and now sat on the couch in my (Sharon's) counseling office with broken hearts, but armed for battle.

"He just doesn't understand my heart!" Yvonne cried in response. "He never has. No matter how much I yell or cry, he just doesn't get it!"

"She has no idea how much I've been hurt by our fighting and harsh words." Tom's voice was thick with emotion. "Yes, maybe I have shut down on the inside, but I've done so just to survive this marriage."

Then something amazing happened, something I've seen happen over and over again with couples. It happens once they reveal to each other what is really at the core of their hearts. Both Tom and Yvonne leaned forward and looked right at me. Almost in unison, they said, "All I ever wanted was to be understood and accepted . . . by him (her)."

Tom and Yvonne sat momentarily motionless. Then they slowly turned to look at each other, their faces gentle and hopeful.

"I just wanted you to be there for me, to understand me, and to value me," Tom whispered.

"That's all I ever wanted too," Yvonne responded. As they embraced, they took a giant leap toward making their marriage a safe haven.

You see, behind all the fighting, yelling, crying, and withdrawing, counselors nearly always find two struggling human beings with broken hearts longing to be understood, accepted, and loved just for who they are. Tom and Yvonne, like all couples, longed to be emotionally connected. They craved a space between them in which they could really, honestly be safe.

SAFE HAVEN MARRIAGE: ROMANCE NOVEL OR REALITY?

If you're a wife, don't be surprised if reading the above stories causes you to feel a deep sense of dissatisfaction in your marriage and an unsettling fear that you may never be able to achieve a safe haven marriage.

And if you're a husband, you may be saying, "Sure, I can see how great it must be to have an emotionally connected, safe relationship. But you don't know my personality. And you can't imagine our history of hurts or how bad our marriage has become. I just could never envision saying to my spouse the things you've quoted, and my spouse would never say them back to me. To be honest, it doesn't sound like something any man could hook up with. It sounds more like a romantic novel than a real-life relationship."

Is that what you're thinking? Before we close this first chapter, please allow us to address some of the questions you may have, as well as some major obstacles that might prevent you and your husband or wife from even beginning your journey.

First things first: Marriages are never safe havens when there is physical or emotional abuse. In such cases, changes beyond the scope of this book are necessary before the journey of fostering a safe haven can begin. Sometimes, years of constant fighting can feel abusive and trusting again difficult. Seeking professional advice can help you discern the difference and initiate the necessary changes.

Second, it is important for you to understand that our suggestions in this book have been scientifically developed and validated in the lives of many couples. They are not just nice ideas. Safe haven couples, as our research demonstrates, are happier, more satisfied, and better able to withstand the storms of life. Their marriages also last longer. These things are true, we believe, because we are working toward the type of marriage that God intends for couples to have.

And we don't have any intention of setting up husbands to do and say things with which they're not comfortable. Nor do we intend to outline a marriage so ideal that wives can only dream about it. We are introducing a way that you and your spouse can emotionally connect and foster a safe haven marriage.

Third, we know from experience that both husbands and wives "feel" their emotions differently. Their expressions of feelings and hurts are also different. A wife might be very verbal and emotionally expressive, while her spouse is inexpressive and more reserved or logical. One spouse might fight for changes, while the other tries to maintain peace and quiet by staying away from any emotion that might start a fight. But despite these differences, remember this: Deep down, your spouse longs to have a close, emotionally safe relationship with you where he feels loved, respected, and understood. *And your spouse wants these things just as much as you do.*

Fourth, you may think that the examples of conversations we share throughout the book don't sound like words real people would ever say—especially the "good" stuff. Well, the truth is that most of these quotes come from a blend of many real-life cases, although we have concealed all identifying information.

But even if you know other people have actually said such things, perhaps you would still feel uneasy saying what we suggest. You needn't sound like anyone but yourself, so please feel free to adjust your words to fit your temperament. Try to understand the point that is being made, and then shape the conversation we offer as an example to fit the way you and your spouse talk. There is no one right way to say anything. Just make sure your words are meaningful to you and your spouse.

Fifth, we accept the fact that for many of our readers at this point, a safe haven marriage may seem impossible to achieve. The hurt and pain that come from being emotionally disconnected for many years can leave deep scars of loneliness, unhappiness, and disappointment. It may be that even as you read you are symbolically holding these hurts in your hand and wondering if you could ever get over them and become emotionally connected again. You might be thinking, *Is this how I want to live for the rest of my life? Don't I deserve to find someone who understands me and values me, and with whom I can be emotionally connected?*

Staying married and working on your marriage may be a risk, but so is walking away from it. Choosing to try again puts you back in a vulnerable place, but so does casting yourself upon unsheltered waters. We fully accept that we are asking you to take further risks. Perhaps you are not sure if your spouse will gain the sort of understanding necessary to build a safe haven marriage. Our response? *You* be the first to change. You'll be a better person for it and a better spouse as well.

Fostering a close emotional connection and working toward a healthy relationship is very possible, no matter how bad your marriage may seem to be. God will hear the cry of your hurting and lonely heart. He will meet you where you are.

Of course, everyone isn't in the same circumstances. Some of you may have strong marriages. Others may have just started on your marital journey and yearn to make it as strong as possible and to avoid the mistakes of others. Whatever your situation, it is our prayer that God will use this book, along with the people and resources in your life, to heal and strengthen your marriage by making it safer than ever. Listen to what one couple who have been successful in their efforts told us.

"I can trust him with my heart. Oh, he is human and so am I. We have had to forgive each other many times, but through it all I can trust him with my heart. I know he trusts me with his" (Gloria, age seventy-two).

"Through thick and thin we have been there for each other. She is my best friend, my confidante. My life is richer because we have shared our lives and hearts together" (Gloria's husband, age seventy-four).

BEFORE WE BEGIN

We hope you are encouraged and ready to begin. Let's take a look at what you can expect in the pages that follow.

As you will see, we define distressed marriages as those where spouses are no longer emotionally connected in a secure and loving way. Far more important than what you and your spouse fight about is whether your fights leave you emotionally disconnected. Anger, disappointment, hurt, frustration, sadness, fear, and resentment can trigger stormy and destructive fighting patterns. These patterns include cycles of criticizing, arguing, pursuing, blaming, defending, and withdrawing—cycles that leave couples unable to offer comfort and safety to each other.

We believe that our approach to healing marriages is far different from what is presented in typical marriage self-help books. We will help you and your spouse gain a clearer perspective of your conflicts, your emotions, and your inner needs and longings. As you are able to recognize your destructive cycles and understand the emotions that fuel them, you will have greater understanding and compassion for one another.

Remember that in the midst of all your fighting, *both you and your spouse long to have a safe place for your hearts.* All your arguments happen because each of you longs to be seen, understood, and valued. Acceptance of each other's differences, feelings, and needs will offer a new way of experiencing each other. This will allow you to develop a new interactional cycle, along with being able to more easily exit and recover from the old cycle. You'll learn to deal with disagreements in your marriage in ways that do not leave you emotionally disconnected. Instead, the connection between you and your spouse will become more caring and secure, and you will experience your marriage as a safe haven.

IN SEARCH OF A SAFE HAVEN

So that you will have a general idea of the journey you will be taking with us through this book, here is a brief overview:

First, we will outline the three key aspects of a safe haven marriage and present to you an abbreviated version of the Haven of Safety Scale, so you can assess how things are going for you and your spouse.

Second, we will provide a general description of a counseling tool called the attachment theory, and you will soon come to appreciate its importance. It is the basic springboard for the approach we will take throughout this book. We hope you'll develop a working knowledge of how it can strengthen your marriage. By the time you've read the last page, you should also be able to apply this model to other relationships in your life, including those with your parents, children, and friends.

Third, we will outline the most destructive emotions and interactional patterns in which couples get stuck. We will show you how your emotions can set in motion the negative interactional patterns that keep you and your spouse stuck and emotionally disconnected.

Fourth, with these ideas in mind, we will show you and your spouse how to heal your broken bonds. The tools we provide will help you restore the emotional safety of your marriage whenever it is disrupted. It would be remiss of us not to point out that the journey toward a safe haven marriage, while absolutely within reach of all, is not without pitfalls and obstacles. It is just as crucial that you know how to recover from a disrupted emotional connection as it is to create that bond in the first place.

REFLECTION QUESTIONS

1. In the midst of all the fighting and arguing that goes on between you and your spouse, what do you each long for?

2. Are you a safe haven for your spouse's heart? Do the things you say and do reflect that?

3. What has been your part in shaping your marriage relationship? What have you and your spouse contributed to the current state of your marriage?

4. What would be the risk of softening your heart and opening up to your spouse?

5. What will hinder you from growing and learning how to do things differently in your marriage? Is it pride or stubbornness? Because you feel sure you are right and your spouse is wrong? Because you feel nothing will change anyway? Because no matter what you do it seems to make no difference?

Chapter 2

OBSTACLES TO A
SAFE CONNECTION

*I long for you, but you are not there. I fear that we will never find
our way back together before we irrevocably wound each other with
our fights.*

—ANONYMOUS CLIENT

*A*s we have already pointed out, couples were never meant to go
through life alone, to endure their married lives without a safe haven.
And yet many husbands and wives find themselves emotionally disconnected.
A husband may love his wife; he may even appreciate many aspects of her personality. A wife may even be glad that she married her husband and would
choose him again if she had it to do all over again. Yet deep down they both
know something is missing. They find themselves unable to turn toward each
other and to discover there a safe place for their feelings, dreams, and hurts.
Fights keep hurts alive between them, preventing them from healing and
restoring their emotional connection.

Consider Doug and Beth, for instance.

Doug pulled up the covers and climbed into bed. Snuggling under the
blankets, he turned toward his wife. Beth fluffed the pillow under her head,
gave a deep sigh, and nestled her body into the mattress, giving the signal,
"I'm down for the night, so don't even think of touching me, fella!"

Beth was as cold as ice. Doug might just as well have curled up in the freezer. Lying there, he longed to reach out and draw her to his body. He wanted so much for the fight to be over, to hold his wife and reconnect their bond. But he dared not make any move toward her because it would only be interpreted as sexual. How could he blame her? After all, that was what she had accused him of earlier that day! *"All you want from me is sex!"* What a hurtful jab! So there he lay in his isolation chamber, hoping and praying that Beth would make some initial gesture toward him. Finally he rolled over, heart aching, closing his eyes to get rid of the tears and to try to fall asleep.

Opening her eyes, Beth tried to turn her head slowly without Doug's noticing. *Why doesn't he just reach out and hold me?* she wondered. *Why doesn't he do something to reassure me that, no matter how bad the fight was, everything will be okay?* She waited for him to take the initiative—it was always easier that way. Slowly she turned her head back and finally fell asleep, her tears caught in her throat.

While both Doug and Beth longed to reconnect, neither of them was willing to cross the invisible line in the middle of their bed. Experience had taught them it wasn't safe for either of them to do that. Needless to say, both woke up the next day weary and with even less tolerance and patience to help them cope with their tension. They were fighting a losing battle, and an unnecessary one.

Too many couples have resigned themselves to marriages much like Doug and Beth's. They accept the fact that their spouse is emotionally unavailable, even though they both long for an emotional connection. Wives have often said to me, "I have been married for many years and my husband is a good man. But he just does not know how to listen to my feelings and connect with me emotionally. I push my husband to share more of himself, but I have learned that he just can't be there for me the way I want him to."

This may be an accurate description of how men behave, but it does not mean that men don't long for this form of intimacy. I (Arch) can assure you that they do. They just can't always find the right way to do it or the precise words to express this yearning.

When husbands do find the words and the courage to express themselves, they usually cry out, "I would love to be *closer* to my wife. Yes, often it is sex that helps me to connect with her, but this gesture on my part is so often misinterpreted that sometimes I don't even want to have sex. It just does not feel safe for me to get close to my wife. I feel that no matter how hard I try, it just isn't good enough. It seems that she is exceptionally emotionally reactive and always upset with me, so I simply protect my heart and withdraw. I love my wife very much, and I long for her to know and understand me. I just don't always know how to make it happen."

We know exactly how you feel. Hopefully, we will be able to help you get past this impasse.

THE PRIMARY PREDICTOR OF DIVORCE

Researchers in the field of family psychology, such as well-known marital researcher John Gottman, have repeatedly confirmed the key predictors of divorce. Before you continue reading, pause here and make a list of what factors you believe can predict divorce. A large age difference between the partners? Possibly, since there could be large generational differences. Or could it be that both spouses come from divorced families? Maybe. Some have suggested this might be a factor. However, since both my brother and I (Arch) come from divorced families and neither of us is divorced, I don't think this is a major factor.

Well, most of you are probably thinking that "fighting all the time" must be a certain predictor of divorce, aren't you? It's the most obvious one that comes to mind. If a couple has many incompatibilities or argues a lot, you might expect that they would be heading toward divorce court soon after the honeymoon. Well, this is not what the research shows.

What the research does show is that *fighting—and by this we mean arguments and disagreements, not physical encounters—is not necessarily hazardous to a marriage.* Our work with troubled marriages confirms this observation. Most couples' arguments and disagreements are rooted in fundamental differences of background, lifestyle, personality, or values and can't be resolved anyway. Disagreements help spouses find a way around these differences.

For instance, one study showed that the most common issues that couples fought over in the early stage of marriage were the same issues they were still fighting over four years later. But John Gottman's research found that it wasn't the content of arguments that predicted divorce, but the *emotional disengagement* that accompanies these fights. In other words, as long as couples remain emotionally connected, their marriages can survive until they find a way around their differences.

Gottman measured a couple's marital satisfaction level and then several years later measured the level again. The couples who had divorced during this period were already emotionally disengaged and withdrawn at the beginning of the study. They had been unable to repair their relationship when they fought or argued. When difficulties came, they turned away from each other instead of toward each other. Their marriages were filled with negativity and failed attempts to connect. They lost all hope that things would change. And they chose to end the vicious fighting cycle by divorcing.

Those whose marriages survived were those who were more connected to begin with and remained connected to the end.

That's right, the number one predictor for divorce is *emotional disconnection,* not fighting. It stands to reason that you won't turn to your spouse for emotional support if the relationship isn't emotionally safe for you to do so. You might struggle to get your partner to understand you and have a lot of disagreements, but if you have a way to emotionally reconnect, preferably quickly, you and your spouse can survive such battles, even grow from them. Continued fighting without the ability to emotionally reconnect will eventually put your marriage at risk.

WHAT PREVENTS YOU AND YOUR SPOUSE FROM EMOTIONALLY CONNECTING?

Why don't husbands and wives connect emotionally? And why don't they make a reconnection when their emotional bond is broken? Let's consider some possible reasons.

Busyness of Life

Various seasons of life affect the amount of time, energy, emotional capacity, and leftover attention you and your spouse have for each other. When you have little kids at home, they consume all the available, spare energy. The time that the wife must expend caring for children, supervising homework, organizing extracurricular activities, and then taking care of the house leaves little time (never mind energy) at the end of the day to spend bonding with her husband. Meanwhile, most husbands are exhausted by the demands of a highly competitive world, in which they feel they must succeed to provide for their family. Couples in this season of life can easily become ships that just barely pass in the night!

Other demanding "seasons" may include illness, returning to school to earn a degree, moving, changing jobs, and family restructuring (births; deaths; children leaving home, returning home, or marrying; aging parents, to name a few). These seasons demand emotional focus and drain us physically, mentally, and emotionally. And it is precisely at these times, when you require greater support and availability from your spouse, that your spouse probably doesn't have the energy or time to give it. Hot emotions often arise, fueling fights and arguments and leaving you and your spouse constantly hurt and disconnected. This adds strain to a marriage. How can you be there for each other when you are rushed, depleted, and needing more support than you can offer in return? And all the remaining energy you have is often spent fighting and arguing.

What can we do about such busyness? I don't know how many times we have dealt with couples over this issue. The solution demands that you carefully review your separate schedules and *build in* time for each other. Effective time management, forcing yourselves to say no to extra demands from outside the family, and generally not taking on any activity that is not absolutely essential can go a long way toward a solution.

You may also have to make a few tough choices. I (Arch) have challenged high-pressured businessmen and -women to choose between their marriages and how much success is necessary in a career. Some have chosen to step down to a lesser (yet still adequate) income for a season, just for the sake of getting a family life.

Past Hurts and Vulnerable Places

To bond with my son when he was young, he and I (Sharon) started taking karate together. One day while sparring and doing our karate moves, my son twisted my body around his leg while holding on to my wrist. He then somersaulted me onto the mat, very proud of his move and ability to overpower me. But I paid a price for this time spent bonding. I ended up with a bad knee and a weak wrist. Now, each time I move the wrong way or pick up something heavy, that old injury comes back to hurt and haunt me. I subsequently quit karate lessons, while my son Vincent has continued and is now approaching his black belt.

My story illustrates that old emotional injuries stay with us and can come back to haunt us. Often we don't know we have them until some pressure is applied in just the exact spot. Then a sudden surge of pain reveals the weakness created by the wound. These susceptible spots become our *vulnerable places*. In the emotional side of our lives we also have vulnerable places, where we have been hurt or wounded. These are just as real and painful as any physical area that has become sensitized to the touch.

In the next three chapters, we will show how we can be emotionally wounded and how emotional damage can occur over the course of our lives. In this book, we only want to deal with childhood experiences—related to parents, caretakers, or other significant people in your upbringing who were not sensitive to your needs and did not respond to you in caring ways—that have caused vulnerable places in your marriage. These are important issues in helping you understand why you respond the way you do when your spouse does something that touches these vulnerable, emotional places.

Here are a couple of examples: If your parents divorced and you suffered through years of being shunted back and forth in a custody battle, you may be vulnerable to feelings of being abandoned. Or if your father shamed you whenever you expressed sadness or weakness, you might now be vulnerable to rejection or criticism. By recognizing what your vulnerable places are, you become more aware of them when they are touched. You can remind yourself that the reason you react in a certain way is not due to anything that is happening right now, but to something that happened a long time ago. Then you can understand how you react to your spouse and make sense of what is happening in your relationship today.

Disappointed . . . Again!

"That really was the last straw! The sink is overflowing with dirty dishes and he expects me to come home and prepare supper under these conditions? He's supposed to clean up the dishes, because he gets home before I do! I've had to put up with his inconsideration and procrastination for years, but this time I just snapped. I am sick and tired of it. It adds too much emotional tension to my already hectic life."

This is how one client complained about a crisis in her marriage, a crisis that was born out of a sequence of small and seemingly inconsequential things. But a constant stream of little disappointments, dripping incessantly against a rock, can erode the rock away. Constant irritations can tear away at your marriage and prevent a safe haven from developing. Those minor daily slights and petty, frequent criticisms can all accumulate. Eventually they will wear away the cartilage of your heart, so that every time it beats it hurts.

Emotional disconnection doesn't require an emotional earthquake. Just pile on the critical comments, insensitive remarks, and irritating acts, whether intentional or unintentional, and you can break your partner's heart. Not much more than a flat-toned hello from your spouse after you've waited all day to see him, a kiss that did not seem warm, a hand touched then quickly pulled away, unwillingness to stop for a hug, failure to help get the kids up and ready in time for school, the thoughtlessness of not putting the dirty dishes in the sink, clothes left in the hallway, or not having time to listen when a listening ear is desperately needed—all these can do deep damage, one bit at a time.

Sometimes these little hurts can be brushed off or swept under the rug. But hurts that are not talked through or don't provide opportunities for apologies build upon one another. Although each incident may be insignificant and easily explained away, the accumulation of slights cannot easily be overlooked.

Little hurts can take on a life of their own. They can come to mean, "You don't care about me; you don't want to know me, understand me, respect me, or love me. Therefore, there is no way I can trust you with my heart. It isn't safe!"

Unresolved Relationship Hurts

Not all hurting comes in small, insignificant doses. Sometimes it comes in the form of big, walloping wounds. "We have never resolved some big issues that occurred early in our marriage, and they still linger. It is hard to attend to the little shadows that bother us now when we haven't healed the storms of our past hurts," Frank and Helen admitted in therapy.

Years before, Frank had lost his job, and Helen had gone back to work right after giving birth to her second baby. Then her mother got cancer. Helen had to quit her job so she could take care of her ill parents. By then Frank had started a new job and didn't feel very secure in it, so he became furious at his wife. He felt Helen should have continued working so they could gain some financial security and build up a safety net. Helen's other family members could take care of her parents, he thought.

Helen was already angry that she'd had to go to work and leave her newborn baby with somebody else. She deeply regretted missing out on those early months. And now her husband's attitude just made matters worse. For a long time they barely spoke at all and Helen remained adamant about not working. Then, months later, she found out she was pregnant again.

"It's now been ten years since all that happened," Helen explains, "but that season of chaos and bitter anger between us has never really been resolved. We argue a lot about it even now, and we throw a lot of 'who did what' into each other's faces. But it just doesn't bring us close together again. It's as if permanent damage has been done to our marriage relationship."

Abdul and Janice began to have trouble after Abdul was promoted to a new and more demanding career position, which took him away from home several times a month. This left Janice alone with their children, even during some critical illnesses. For five years, Abdul was gone, tired, or otherwise unable to emotionally connect with Janice.

Their times together consisted of Janice criticizing Abdul for not being there and pushing him to be more involved in the family. Abdul's reaction was to shut Janice out. The more Abdul shut her out, the more Janice pursued and pushed for his attention. Abdul and Janice were unable to spend time talking and sharing their life together, so he had no idea what her days with the kids were like. Consequently, he didn't have much empathy when she complained. At the same time, Janice did not understand Abdul's business world, and since he refused to talk to her about it, she felt that his work was a threat—the destroyer of their family. The conflict through these important family development years left them deeply scarred emotionally, despite the fact that they continued to love each other dearly.

All too often, situations like Abdul and Janice's lead to extramarital affairs, when one partner seeks another person for emotional support. The impact of serious violations of trust, as in affairs, or of prolonged hostility and hurt, cannot be removed easily. (Such cases are beyond the reach of self-help, and we strongly advise couples with such hurts to seek competent marriage counseling.) Whatever you do, don't allow your hurts to remain unresolved! The longer you leave them, the harder you will have to work to restore emotional connection to your relationship.

Not There When I Need You Most

The problem in a marriage may not be the accumulation of small incidents or the catastrophic betrayal of trust that gets in the way of building a safe haven marriage. It may be the result of some specific event or events that served as a negative turning point in a couple's relationship. Usually it lies in a profound awareness that your partner just wasn't there for you when you really needed him.

Events or turning points like this change the way one spouse views the other in terms of emotional safety. Such incidents are likely to have left you feeling alone, abandoned, or betrayed. Couples with this kind of issue are often able to go back and review their relationship, identifying the events that marked the beginning of their relationship problems. Some wounds may even date back to when the couple were dating.

Matt remembers all too clearly that two weeks before getting married to Ellen, she stayed out all night. Ellen said she had gone out with an old high-school friend, and since it got late, she'd just spent the night at her friend's apartment. It was no big deal to her.

Matt never believed Ellen. He felt there was more to her story, although he just wasn't quite sure what. Somehow he felt betrayed. He never made an issue of it at the time, but a sense of suspicion and feelings of untrustworthiness began to grow within him, tangling themselves around eighteen years of marriage. For all those years, Ellen was able to feel her husband's distance, his constant monitoring of her activities, and his habit of keeping track of all her comings and goings.

Along similar lines, Carrie remembers when her husband Dale's family made a joke about the weight she had gained after her first child.

"Dale laughed with them!" she told me tearfully. "And then he said, 'Yeah, I got more than what I started with,' and then laughed. He did not stand up for me! I was so hurt. I tried to tell him how it hurt me for months afterward, but he just told me not to be so sensitive and to drop the whole thing. He said no one meant anything by it. He just couldn't take my side. From that point, something changed inside of me."

For Carrie, Dale's inability or unwillingness to defend her in front of his family caused her to feel alone and abandoned. It triggered a fear inside her that she could never really trust Dale again and that she would ultimately have to take care of herself—a pretty lonely position.

To this day Dale has no idea why this incident was so hurtful to Carrie, and Carrie has never been able to come to the place of forgiveness.

Many of the hurts we don't deserve cannot be undone, nor can we expect those who hurt us to come forward and ask for our forgiveness. Since forgiveness is the only way out of the prison of resentment, we are trapped until we take steps to effect forgiveness.

Many of the hurts we experience are about taking the risk of trusting the other person with our heart again. We pull back to protect ourselves, and we promise never to be vulnerable or risk trusting again. We don't feel emotionally safe.

Today, Carrie still brings up Dale's betrayal during fights and whenever she feels Dale is again not there for her. Dale spends most of his time defending himself and telling Carrie over and over again that it is ridiculous for her to still hold the incident against him.

These incidences, for obvious reasons, are called betrayals of trust. A sense of security has been shattered, and one or the other spouse is no longer viewed as emotionally safe. We call the consequences of such betrayals of trust *heart injuries,* because that is precisely what they are. Since heart injuries are very common and often are very destructive to building a safe haven marriage, we will outline the process of healing in more detail in chapter 9.

FAMILY OF ORIGIN ISSUES AND LIFESTYLE PREFERENCES

Each of us comes into marriage with a definite view of how life ought to be lived and how things should unfold. In your family, through your parents' teaching and example, you learned how to deal with anger and sadness, how to ask for your needs to be met, how to problem-solve, how to fight, how to show love, and how to deal with difficulties. Subtly but surely, you received an internal blueprint for how life should be lived.

For example, Barbara's family always dealt with disagreements head-on and aired their grievances. Her husband Rick's family was very different. They might have "felt something in the air," but they never really talked about it. Instead, they would each go their separate ways and come back together when the air had cleared. Today, when Barbara voices her dissatisfaction about something, she wants a back-and-forth discussion about the issues. But when Rick senses a wave of emotion rising, he's out the door and out of the conversation.

Jeremy is a morning person, rising early to start each day with renewed energy and zest—just like his parents. His wife, Angela, is a night person who comes from a family of artists and writers in which the best times for creativity and conversations were the wee hours of the morning. In her view, mornings are for sleeping and definitely not for conversing. She stays up late and gets her second wind just before midnight. Jeremy views Angela's nightlife as selfish and insensitive; he feels Angela is simply avoiding him. She hates the noise he makes in the morning and feels that he is manipulating her by crashing around in the bedroom and bathroom. Their obvious lifestyle differences cause many arguments.

Other differences that are sources of conflict are:

- You refuel with people and are energized by activity while your spouse is an introvert and longs for time alone to refuel and regroup.

- You are more thrifty and value a penny saved while your spouse values making life more comfortable and enjoyable now.
- You are more open-minded, adventurous, and blaze your own trail while your spouse tends to follow a set course between the established lines.

The more differences there are between your family background and lifestyle preferences and those of your spouse, the more likely you are to disagree and have conflict. And as with all differences, these often come to mean, "You are not there for me. You don't care about me." Family and lifestyle differences may even be viewed as moral issues: "It's wrong for you to do it that way." Or as deep inadequacies: "If you were a better person, you wouldn't do it that way." But they eventually boil down to an all too familiar belief—"If you really understood and loved me, you wouldn't do it that way."

Creating and sustaining an emotional connection with your spouse is the most important goal of your marriage. Once that connection is in place, neither the busyness of life, past hurts and disappointments, perceived betrayals, nor differences in family background and lifestyle will have the power to do serious damage to your safe haven. In the next chapter, we'll take a look at some building blocks that will help you construct the marriage of your dreams.

REFLECTION QUESTIONS

1. Review the beginning of your relationship. How did you meet, what were your first impressions of each other, how did you grow to fall in love and decide to marry?

2. On a piece of paper, draw a time line of your marital relationship. What were the early years in your marriage like? Over the years of your marriage, when were the good seasons and when were the rough seasons? Place a "W" next to the years that were difficult and were your "winters" and an "S" next to the years that were warm and good like "summers."

3. What events or seasons in your marriage defined your marriage as a safe haven or redefined it as an unsafe place for your heart?

4. Is your relationship a safe haven now? If so, what makes it so? What enables you and your spouse to stay (or not stay) emotionally connected?

5. What are the strengths of your marriage? What are your and your spouse's personality strengths?

Chapter 3

IS YOUR MARRIAGE
A SAFE HAVEN?

Right here in your arms is the safest place.
—LEANN RIMES, "THE SAFEST PLACE"

*U*npleasant as they are, we've seen that arguments are not the real culprits in putting marriages at risk for breakup. The bigger issue is whether a couple is able to stay emotionally connected or can find a way to quickly reconnect if their connection is broken. In this chapter, we will take a closer look at three essential building blocks for a safe haven marriage and how each can impact your relationship. We will also define "clarification communication" and consider how important it is to fostering a safe haven. And we will introduce an abbreviated copy of the Haven of Safety Scale, a tool we have developed to help you assess to what extent you experience each other as a safe haven.

YOU HOLD MY HEART AND I HOLD YOURS

I (Arch) grew up in South Africa, where we speak a second language called Afrikaans, a derivative of Dutch. It is a very expressive language, and many phrases are far more colorful than in English. For instance, the phrase "I love you" in Afrikaans is *"Ek het jou lief."* It literally means, "I have your love," or "I have your heart." What a potent statement! When a husband and wife love each other, they literally give their hearts to each other for safekeeping. This is such a delicate, trusting act that any violation or injury of this trust can cause the most painful of reactions.

Imagine taking the very essence of your being—your heart—and placing it in the hands of your spouse. Your heart becomes your mate's to care for, safeguard, cherish, and love. This necessitates a willingness to be vulnerable and take a bold, risky step. If your partner reciprocates, you both have chosen to risk being hurt, rejected, and abandoned. Placing your heart in the hands of another is a giant step of faith. Afterward, you can only wait to see what your spouse will do with your heart. Your desire, of course, is that your spouse will be a safe haven for your heart. And that is your spouse's longing as well.

BUILDING BLOCKS FOR A SAFE HAVEN

Virtually all couples silently ask each other, *Will you be a safe haven for my heart? Can I trust you to be there for me when I reach for you? Will you be emotionally available to me? Will you consider me and respond in the best interest of us both? Despite all our hardships and conflicts, do you really care about and value me?* The answers to these questions are crucial. If your spouse is unable or unwilling to value you, why would you let him or her keep your heart? The fact is, you probably wouldn't. And who can blame you?

What are the key qualities of a safe haven? Is it a list of what to do and what not to do? Are there steps to take, habits to learn, and skills to master? No, a safe haven is not fostered by mastering skills or learning dos and don'ts. To try to create a safe haven that way would be to miss the whole point. The qualities of a safe haven are more about "ways of being" with your spouse. These qualities mean that you are someone with whom your spouse can feel safe, secure; you are someone who sees, loves, accepts, and understands your partner, and vice versa. In this way, understanding grows, empathy is expressed, acceptance is shared, and a willingness to grow and change arises.

When you are able to discover and develop the qualities of a safe haven in your marriage, you and your spouse will begin to experience each other differently, coming together for friendship, conversations, comfort, and fun without reluctance or defensiveness.

The building blocks that our clinical experience and research have shown to be essential to a safe haven marriage are trust, emotional availability, and sensitive responsiveness.

These three building blocks come out of the attachment theory, one of the most important approaches to understanding marriage. Research has shown that these qualities are crucial to building a healthy marriage. However, to make this book readable, we will not clutter our discussion by citing specific studies. The additional reading resources provided in the bibliography will provide adequate support for any research mentioned.

One research project, conducted by Mary Ainsworth, was an important aspect of John Bowlby's development of the attachment theory. This theory demonstrates how important these three qualities are to the relationships between parents and children. Mary Ainsworth observed children in Africa and America to discover how the mother-child relationship impacted the development of children. She carefully observed how mothers responded to their children in stressful situations. She discovered that the emotional health and well-being of a child was greatly affected by the mother's emotional accessibility and availability, and by whether the mother responded to her child with care and concern.

The children who fared the best were those whose mothers were not only physically available, but also emotionally available. They were attuned to their child's needs and responded with sensitivity, concern, and consideration. The mother was a safe haven. The child knew where to turn for comfort. After further research several decades later, the same three qualities and principles were shown to be crucial to fostering a safe haven between marital couples.

The relationship between you and your spouse is the most precious relationship in your life. It is your harbor, your nest, in which you find safety, love, and acceptance and the place from which you draw energy to face the world. It is no wonder that your relationship needs to be a safe haven where you can trust that the person you love will be attuned to your needs, emotionally available and accessible, and will respond to you in a way that is sensitive and considerate, keeping the best interest of the relationship at heart.

THE SAFE HAVEN TRIPOD

These building blocks for a safe haven form a sort of tripod—if one is missing, the whole haven of safety is likely to be impacted. Let's look at them one at a time.

Trust

The first leg of the safe haven tripod is *trust*. Trust has been defined in many different ways. There is *truthfulness trust* (your partner can be relied upon to always tell you the truth) and *judgment trust* (your partner can be relied upon to make good judgment calls). But the two aspects of trust that we will focus on here are *reliability trust* and *heart trust,* the latter being the most important.

1. Reliability Trust. When you have reliability trust, you have the assurance that your spouse will be dependable, on time, honest, and truthful. This kind of trust means that you and your partner will keep your word to each other, and you will do what you say when you say you'll do it. In marriage you should be able to trust your spouse with your money, body, future, possessions, dreams, goals, and secrets. In all that is important to them, spouses ought to be able to know that their partners will be respectful, dependable, responsible, and reliable. This is *reliability trust.*

How does reliability trust develop? It is built through experience. For example, when your wife picks up the kids from soccer practice on time, just as she promised, you don't have to worry about it or do it yourself later. A seed of reliability trust has been planted. From experience, you trust that your spouse will not spend the last penny in your bank account without first checking with you. And when your husband says that he will be late because he is stuck on the freeway because of an accident, you trust that he is telling the truth.

On the other hand, trust erodes when we fail to follow through on our promises. It suffers when we sugarcoat truth, putting an unpleasant reality in a better light in hopes our spouse will not get upset. Or when we habitually exaggerate and don't care about getting the facts right. How can a spouse lean on and trust a partner who often fudges the truth?

When mistrust infiltrates a marriage, both husband and wife begin to question each other in regard to where they were, who they were with, and what they did. This happens not always in terms of fidelity, but with money, business dealings, decision making, use of time, and caring for the children. Mistrust begins a pattern of relating that keeps spouses emotionally protected and one step away from each other.

Both husband and wife also need to know that they can trust each other to meet family obligations. The wife needs to know that the husband will be the caretaker, spiritual leader, and gatekeeper of the family and home. And the husband needs to trust that his wife will be the nurturer, supporter, and helpmate in all areas of the family. Both need assurance that the other will work hard and consistently, so the family is provided for and the children are looked after. Each needs to be assured that the other will do his part faithfully, in a way they have mutually agreed upon.

Both husbands and wives long to know that their spouse will turn to God for wisdom in their decisions when caring for the family. Oftentimes a wife will have a difficult time placing her whole life into the hands of her husband because the risk seems so great. And if he is flirtatious, shifts the finances around in secrecy, is temperamental, procrastinates, lets things slip through the cracks, or is always seeking fun for himself, she has an even worse time trusting and following his leadership and decisions. She will always question him, nag him, and withhold her heart from him.

Sometimes reliability trust is developed simply because of differences in personality. For instance, a wife may be easygoing, not a clock watcher, and therefore always late. Her husband may be very rigid about time. He will distrust her and maybe consider her irresponsible and inconsiderate, even though she is a trustworthy person in the context of her personality. She will, in turn, distrust him because he always criticizes her lack of punctuality and never sees her heart's intent.

Reliability distrust—whether warranted or unwarranted—causes husbands and wives to pull back emotionally and be overly self-protective. Sometimes the wife or the husband has done something in the past to break trust or give reason for suspicion. Other times mistrust is based not on what a spouse has done or not done, but on wounds that have been brought into the relationship. If a wife had a volatile father who was unpredictable, or a husband had a mother who was controlling and untrustworthy, then each spouse will bring the resulting fears and mistrust into the marriage. You need to be sensitive to your own as well as your spouse's wounds and how they impact the way you relate. This way you can begin to break the old mistrust patterns and together share experiences that rebuild trust. Be patient. Rebuilding trust after it is broken takes time.

2. Heart Trust. There is another kind of trust that is of even greater importance to a safe haven marriage. It is called *heart trust.* This means you are convinced, despite all the fights and storms you've had in your marriage and no matter what may happen between the two of you, that your spouse will always care for you and value you. This is the deepest level of trust the human heart can give or receive. This is the ultimate in emotional security. You are able to say to your spouse, "I trust you with my heart."

Heart trust occurs when you believe that your spouse is genuinely interested in your welfare and in what is best for the relationship. You perceive your spouse to be kind, generous, thoughtful, considerate, and having your well-being in mind at all times. The sentiment is, "My spouse is a good person and has good intentions. I know I can trust my spouse with my heart."

The faith that your partner will act in loving and caring ways, no matter what the future holds, is the center beam that holds up your safe haven. Research has found that heart trust, or faith in one's spouse to be caring and loving, predicts how well a couple will do in marital counseling. If a couple comes to counseling and does not have faith that, despite how much they fight, their spouse will be caring and loving, they will have a difficult time rebuilding their marriage through therapy. And it's worth noting that wives have a harder time rebuilding heart trust than husbands.

A partner who does not trust her spouse will be less likely to ask for and give support. Without trust, a couple is unwilling to share one another's vulnerabilities, needs, and hurts. This promotes patterns of criticism, of trying to force each other to change, of reading negative intentions into the choices and behaviors of one's spouse, or of defensiveness and self-protection. These habits keep couples emotionally disconnected.

We don't want you to be become too disheartened here. If your marriage has suffered an affair or other serious kind of betrayal, there *is* hope. You may, even now, be saying to your spouse, "I'll never trust you again! I will never again risk putting my heart in your hands just so you can step all over it!" In reality, relationships can and do heal after affairs and other betrayals. Even when trust is shattered, it can be rebuilt. No marital wound is beyond God's ability to heal and restore. Many a marriage that has been scarred by an affair or other breaches in trust has been restored because both spouses were willing to risk loving again. We will discuss this later in the book.

Emotional Availability

Does this sound like a familiar scenario?

Wife: "Honey, you won't believe what happened to me today. . . ." Sees husband reading mail and hesitates. "Oh, did I catch you at a bad time?"

Husband, reading his mail intently: "No. What happened?"

Wife: "Well, it was rather incredible, really . . . oh, I can see you are busy. But I just wanted to tell you . . ."

Husband: "No, really, what happened?" Husband shuffles letters, occasionally glancing up at his wife.

Wife: "Oh, forget it; go through your mail."

Husband: "What? You came in and interrupted me. I put my mail down; now are you going to tell me or not?"

Wife turns on her heel and storms out of the room.

Sad to say, in too many marriages, this is a familiar scene.

There is a very popular British television comedy series on public television called *Keeping Up Appearances*. The main character is Hyacinth, a stuffy, middle-aged lady who has to "keep up appearances" so as to be respected by all. She's married to long-suffering and saintly Richard, whom everyone pities. In one episode, Richard has been devastated by news that he has to take early retirement. He wants so desperately to share this depressing news with Hyacinth, and to talk about how they'll have to somehow coexist with his being retired.

"We have to talk about it, Hyacinth," he ventures. "I know you never listen to me, but we really have to talk about it."

Hyacinth, fiddling with the white, slimline telephone she thinks every neighbor envies, responds, "That's nice, dear." She moves on to make a call, complaining that her neighbor gets more mail than she does. In fact, everyone who tries to tell her anything personal gets her "That's nice, dear," no matter what the crisis or tragedy. Needless to say, you really come to admire Richard for sticking with the epitome of the trustworthy but emotionally unavailable wife.

In safe haven marriages, spouses are not only physically available, but they make their hearts available to each other as well. Emotional availability, therefore, is the second leg of the tripod that supports safe haven marriages.

You see, it is possible for a spouse to be thoroughly trustworthy—*but not physically or emotionally available.* Result? The safety of the marriage is undermined. One wife put it this way: "I've always been able to trust my husband. From the earliest dating days to the present, I've always been able to trust him to do what he promises. I've never had reason to believe he isn't faithful. But he is *never available* to the kids or me when we need him. His work consumes him. He has too many other distractions. It's like we live separate lives!"

To be emotionally available is to turn your attention toward your wife whenever she needs you. It is to allow not only your ears and your mind, but also your heart to be there for her. To be emotionally available means that you give your husband your full attention and interest whenever you are with him. When he needs to share his thoughts or ideas with you, your heart is eager and ready to listen with full attention and concern. Does that sound like a tall order? Maybe so. Maybe it even sounds impossible. But nothing can replace emotional availability in marriage.

When your spouse needs you, you have to be available, physically and emotionally. You have to be where your spouse can find you. On a regular basis you should set up time to build your relationship just as you would build a career or try to please a boss. In this way you are each able to turn toward the other when you need it the most, and experience the security and pleasure of a safe haven.

What does research have to tell us here? Studies have found that marital satisfaction is highly correlated with whether a person perceives a spouse to be emotionally or psychologically available to them. If one spouse believes that the other is willing to turn her full attention toward him, he will experience his marriage as satisfying. Husbands who had confidence that their wives would be emotionally available were less rejecting and more supportive when they were problem-solving. These studies also showed that wives felt more assured of themselves when their husbands listened attentively to them during problem-solving discussions. Those are powerful findings. You can actually build your spouse's self-esteem and help her or him better cope with stress by being more supportive.

Let us put this in some perspective. Inevitably, there will be times when one or the other partner is not available emotionally for short periods of time— during especially busy days, times of illness, extended family crises, or business trips. This need not be hurtful or injurious to your safe haven. It is a consistent pattern of unavailability that becomes damaging. If a wife is consistently not there for her husband, or if a wife is rebuffed in repeated attempts to get her husband's attention, this is when hurt, disappointment, and anger set in and take over the marriage.

What undermines emotional availability? Take a moment to review the following reasons that you and your spouse may not be emotionally available and accessible to each other:

1. Discomfort with Closeness. For some spouses, giving one another their full attention holds the potential to be hurtful and is draining. They feel overwhelmed and uncomfortable with the closeness. They are more comfortable doing a project, flipping through the television channels, or sharing an event than sitting and gazing into their spouse's eyes. Often they are introverts; they refuel by going inward rather than talking and sharing their thoughts out loud. And conversations about feelings and relationship issues are uncomfortable and feel, well, unnecessary. One spouse or the other is thinking: *What is there to say?*

2. Busy Schedule, Weary Souls. Maybe you are in that time of life when you have a household full of children, and your attention and focus are diverted in many directions. Perhaps you are trying to blend two families. Or you are in the middle of your career, and trying to climb the ladder of success is your only goal.

When does a day ever end? Even if there are no kids at home, obligations at church, work, and family events can keep couples extremely busy and distracted. By the time evening comes, husbands and wives are exhausted. Couples today struggle with an energy crisis: They don't have enough energy left for each other.

I encourage you to count the emotional cost. Examine whether you can make some changes that will help you to be more accessible. Talk it over with a trusted friend or a counselor. There may be something you can change or surrender that can make you more emotionally available.

3. Empty Nest, Empty Conversations. Maybe your kids have just left home and the empty nest has left you feeling like strangers without the lives of your kids to keep you bonded. You've forgotten how to relate to each other without a focus on others. It will be in the best interest of your marriage to evaluate what you can do to begin rebuilding your relationship by dating and courting one another.

4. Upside-Down Priorities. First things first! What are your priorities? Being better organized might help you manage your time, but unless your relationship is given very high priority, nothing is likely to change. The time you save through time management will only be used to distract you somewhere else. So talk to each other about your priorities. When was the last time you sat down and had an in-depth talk? Or went out on a date? Shared a hobby? Many couples come in for counseling as part of their "date night." They view it as a way of staying close and connected.

5. Havens of Resentment. Harboring resentment after fights or disagreements can create an emotional barrier between you and your spouse that keeps you unavailable or inaccessible. Hurts keep your heart superprotected and supersensitive. You stay busy at the office so you don't have to come home and face the emotional distance. Your outside interests are more satisfying since home is always emotionally draining. Why do you think golf is so popular? It's not that everyone who plays it is good at it!

Remember, however, that when outside activities are distractions from your pain, they are nothing more than Band-Aids on your heart's deep wounds. They might work to numb the emotional pain or give you some peace for a while, but then you still have to go home, and the wounds are still there. If you don't turn toward your spouse to heal those wounds and to work through the disconnection, you will get stuck. The fights will continue. Your hearts will remain closed, and your relationship will never become a safe haven.

Sensitive Responsiveness

We call the third leg of the safe haven tripod *sensitive responsiveness*. A partner can be thoroughly trustworthy and available, but just doesn't respond in a sensitive way. One husband put it this way: "I trust my wife with my life. She never wavers. She's home a lot, so she has no problem spending time with me. But when I start to open up, all I get is a critical comment: 'That won't work.' 'Don't do that!' 'What are you doing that for?' 'Why did you say that?' Of course I just stop right there."

When you approach your spouse about some painful event or hot topic in your relationship, how does your partner respond? Assuming he is trustworthy and available, do you feel he gives you his full and undivided attention? Does she respond to you with understanding, even though she may not agree with you? Does he ask for further explanation, before reacting, if what you are saying sounds hurtful or critical? Do you do the same for him?

Are you approachable? Can your spouse approach you with ease? Does he have your full attention as he attempts to articulate his perspective? Are you and your spouse able to listen with warmth and ease and without judging, criticizing, or problem-solving? "I can't believe you said that!" does not build safe haven marriages.

To be sensitively responsive means you can receive your spouse's innermost thoughts, feelings, needs, and desires readily and without judgment. Likewise, your spouse responds to you in a way that makes you feel understood, validated, and cared about. When you feel these positive responses coming from your spouse, you and your spouse are drawn into a closer emotional connection. The emotions between you become safe and inviting. You are free to share revealing information about events in your lives, what you are feeling and experiencing, without fear of rejection, criticism, or disinterest.

Responsiveness also means your spouse is able to weigh his own needs in one hand and your needs in the other and to respond in the best interests of you both. After carefully considering your needs alongside your spouse's, you respond in a kind, benevolent manner that promotes the best interest of the relationship. This kind of sensitive responsiveness creates and maintains a safe haven between you and your spouse. This is the primary message of this book: *A safe haven marriage is what couples long for most.*

It is difficult for couples to be responsive to each other when the relationship is filled with negativity, criticism, and withdrawing. If your husband thinks you are critical or judgmental every time he tries to share his point of view, he will stop approaching you. It makes sense. Why should any spouse open his heart only to be invalidated, criticized, or shut out? Or if your wife is certain you will only dismiss or discount her perspective, she won't gently share her heart.

Even though you may not always agree with your spouse, make yourself available to understand his point of views and opinions. Be sensitive to mood variations—we all have them. So be understanding rather than punishing or rejecting. And give your full attention to your spouse when she is expressing what is important to her. Listen with warmth, showing interest by responding audibly with phrases such as, "Really?" "Then what happened?" "What was that like for you?" To know you can share your heart with the person you love and be totally accepted means that you have a relationship worth coming home to.

What Can Unbalance the Tripod?

Depending upon the early experiences of your life, you will come into adulthood with varying degrees of ability to express trust, availability, and responsiveness. If, as you grew up, you experienced those closest to you as emotionally available, responsive, and sensitive to your needs, then you will expect those who love you to be a constant source of comfort and care. When you marry you'll be able to turn to your spouse for closeness, to share your heart, dreams, needs, and hurts, believing that your spouse will respect and honor these needs. You'll be confident that you will receive their warmth and support. After all, that's what happened throughout your childhood.

However, if you didn't experience a safe haven growing up, then it is very likely that, as you enter marriage, you will feel unsure about your spouse's ability to be there for you. When your spouse says or does something that touches your vulnerability, hot emotions will be triggered and fights will be ignited. You will either pursue your spouse to seize attention and to gain a sense of safety, or you will fail to reach out for your spouse in order to protect yourself. In the next few chapters, we will review this in more detail.

For example, if you have been hurt by the unavailability of someone close to you, you may bring this wound into your marriage. Say your father never showed up at your hockey games or at your open house at school, even though he promised each time that he would. You now long for the attention and support of your husband but always scan the horizon checking to see when he'll disappoint you and let you down. Today, instead of giving people (especially males) the benefit of the doubt, you habitually question their reliability. You doubt whether you can trust others to be available and responsive to your heart's needs.

It's important to learn to recognize the moments when a past vulnerability is being triggered. That's the time to risk moving through your fears of being rejected and risk trusting the love and care your spouse is offering. It might prove helpful, for example, to tell yourself, "I know I've been hurt by my other relationships, but my husband isn't those other people. I need to understand how my past is impacting my present, in order to open my heart and receive the love my spouse is offering."

For whatever reason, you may find yourself constantly examining your relationship for evidence of unreliability or emotional unavailability. Of course, if you look for trouble hard enough, you'll find it. And any inconsistency, even if it is quite innocent, may cause you to become anxious and angry, accusing your partner of being thoughtless, inconsiderate, disrespectful, forgetful, or uncaring. This kind of unwarranted scanning will destroy your ability to lean on and trust your spouse. It will also turn your spouse into a distruster as well. You will both spend your energy trying to protect yourselves from each other's unwarranted accusations.

CLARIFICATION COMMUNICATION

Earlier we mentioned that clarification communication is important in helping to restore a disconnected relationship. When a couple is able to openly communicate with each other, the unavailability or unresponsiveness of either partner can be "clarified," hence the label "clarification communication." Think of it as gathering more information about your spouse's failure to follow through on their commitment, their emotional unavailability, or their unresponsiveness—before jumping to conclusions and reacting. This ability is vitally important to your safe haven marriage. Consider this exchange:

"Your mother is the worst housekeeper."

"How dare you say that about my mother!"

"I can say what I want. Don't tell me how to feel about things."

This conversation got quickly out of hand but could have easily been averted if the spouses had asked for more information about what their partner meant. It could have sounded something like this:

"You said my mother is a bad housekeeper, and you often say that I am just like my mother. So are you saying that I am a terrible housekeeper and that I am a big disappointment to you?"

"No, no. I just wanted to sit on my favorite rocking chair at your mother's house tonight, and she had all her stuff on it. I didn't mean anything about you. I got defensive when you got mad at me and scolded me for saying what I said about your mother."

"No, sorry, I guess I should have asked what you meant by that."

"Yeah, I'm sorry too."

Or think about this scenario: Suppose Jay is sitting on the couch reading his Sunday paper. In walks his wife, Zenith. She has an angry look on her face and plops down on the sofa across from him.

Jay looks up and thinks, *Oh, great! She's mad again. She's always mad about something. Is she mad because I'm reading the newspaper and didn't help with the dishes?*

Jay slams the newspaper into his lap and snaps, "Now what? If you want to pick a fight, I am not in the mood."

Zenith glares at Jay. Her voice drips with sarcasm. "Oh *no*, I wouldn't *dream* of interrupting you while you read the paper. No one bothers Mr. Take-It-Easy on a Sunday afternoon."

Both Jay and Zenith needed to clarify each other's unavailability and seemingly insensitive response. Jay could have thought instead, *She looks upset. Let me see if I can understand what's on her mind.* He could have just as easily asked a clarification question. "You look upset. What's happened?"

Zenith could have then explained her angry entrance by saying, "I just wanted to let you know that the puppy has gotten into the trash again. It would be nice if you could take the trash out right after dinner each night. I've just had to clean it all up again."

And then they could have moved to solving the problem: how to keep trash out of the reach of their puppy. Afterward, they could have enjoyed the rest of the evening together.

If couples are willing to take a few first steps toward open and honest clarification, the restoration of a lost emotional connection becomes easier. In short: Find out what's wrong. Don't be afraid to ask. Get more information about why your spouse is mad or withdrawn, and make it an opportunity to exchange perspectives and to consider your spouse's concerns. Then provide comfort or even offer constructive ways to do things differently.

On the other hand, remember that when you express anger toward your spouse with critical remarks and fail to provide a clear explanation for your frustration, your anger is likely to be interpreted as rejection or as a threat to emotional availability. Your spouse will probably not respond to you with sensitivity.

This is what happened to Brian and Liz as they were driving home from his parents' house. Leaning over to hold her hand, Brian accidentally knocked over Liz's purse, spilling the contents all over the floor. Bending over the backseat to pick up the items, Liz moaned and said, "I can't believe you."

Brian asked Liz, "Are you mad at me?"

Liz answered, "What do you think?"

Brian asked again, "Did I do something to upset you?"

Liz replied, "Can you just drop it?"

Brian fires back, "Fine, if you want to be in a bad mood, go ahead. You are so moody. So unpredictable!"

Not sure why she was mad at him, Brian reacted with defensiveness and anger. Fortunately, Liz caught the beginnings of her sulk and clarified her bad mood. "I am sorry, Brian. I am not mad at you. I just don't know how to deal with your mother's comments about when we are going to have children."

"I'm sorry about what my mom said to you," Brian said quietly. "I should have jumped in and said something, but I didn't. I'm sorry for that too."

Liz reached for Brian's hand.

Our happiest moments come when we feel the safest! Clarifying conversations can lead us in that direction.

IS YOUR RELATIONSHIP A HAVEN OF SAFETY?

Now that we've discussed some important aspects of building a safe haven, let's take a closer look at *your* marriage. Where are you in your relationship? Do you perceive your relationship to be a safe haven?

The following is an extract from a test that was designed by Sharon. It is highly correlated with a popular scale that measures marital satisfaction. In other words, couples who scored low on the Haven of Safety Scale also scored low in marital satisfaction. So if you perceive your spouse to be high on the safe haven scale, then you will most likely experience your marriage as scoring high in marital satisfaction and happiness.

This is an abridged version of the test. The full test is only available for use by marriage therapists. Details on how to obtain the complete scale are provided in Appendix C.

The Haven of Safety Scale is comprised of three sections that cover the tripod we've been discussing in this chapter. First is a subscale for *trust*. Do you trust your spouse to be caring and loving despite what happens in your relationship? Second is a subscale for *emotional availability*. Do you perceive your spouse to be emotionally available to you? Third is a subscale for *responsiveness*. Does your spouse respond to you in a considerate and caring manner?

The way you answer each question in each section will give you an idea of whether you perceive your spouse to be trustworthy, available, or responsive. Carefully review each question because how you answer will give you insight and information in regard to the safety of your relationship or how you and your spouse can grow to be a more safe place for each other. When you consider all three areas—trust, emotional availability, and responsiveness—you come up with an overall picture of how you perceive your spouse as a *haven of safety.*

Abbreviated Haven of Safety Scale[1]
Sharon Hart Morris, Ph.D.

The following questions will help you gain understanding about your marriage. Using the scale below, please *circle* the corresponding number that best fits *how you perceive your spouse.* Read the questions again and *write* on the line the corresponding number that best fits what you think *your spouse would say about you.*

Never	Rarely	Occasionally	More often than not	Most of the time	All the time
0	1	2	3	4	5

TRUST

0 1 2 3 4 5 ___1. My partner is honest and truthful with me.

0 1 2 3 4 5 ___2. I can trust my partner.

0 1 2 3 4 5 ___3. My partner has the best interest of our relationship foremost in his/her mind.

0 1 2 3 4 5 ___4. I can accept the decisions my partner makes in important areas of our relationship.

0 1 2 3 4 5 ___5. My partner is not self-centered or selfish.

0 1 2 3 4 5 ___6. I am certain that my partner will not intentionally hurt me.

If you scored the majority of the items as 3, 4, or 5, then most of the time, if not all the time, your spouse is trustworthy. You believe your spouse will be considerate, thoughtful, unselfish, honest, and reliable. If you scored any of the questions 2, 1, or 0, consider why, as that area of your relationship is of possible concern.

EMOTIONAL AVAILABILITY

0 1 2 3 4 5 ___1. My partner gives me his/her full attention when I need to share what's important to me.

0 1 2 3 4 5 ___2. I can count on my partner to be emotionally accessible when I need him/her.

0 1 2 3 4 5 ___3. I am able to talk openly with my partner about what's important to me.

0 1 2 3 4 5 ___4. We give and receive support from each other with ease.

0 1 2 3 4 5 ___5. My partner is willing to put aside what he/she is doing to spend time with me.

0 1 2 3 4 5 ___6. My partner does not seem to give more [undue] time and attention to things other than our marriage.

If you scored most of the items 3, 4, or 5, then more often than not, if not all the time, your spouse is emotionally available to you. You believe your spouse will give you their attention, be available to you, talk with you, support you, and focus attention on your marriage. If you scored any of the questions 2, 1, or 0, consider why, as that area of your relationship is possibly of concern.

RESPONSIVENESS

0 1 2 3 4 5 ___1. Even though we might have different views, my partner tries to take into consideration my perspective.

0 1 2 3 4 5 ___2. I do not have to walk on eggshells around my partner.

0 1 2 3 4 5 ___3. When we are in conflict, my partner is still able to respond in a considerate way.

0 1 2 3 4 5 ___4. When making important decisions, I know my partner will think through my point of view.

0 1 2 3 4 5 ___5. My partner is understanding of my moods and feelings.

0 1 2 3 4 5 ___6. We are able to constructively resolve our relationship hurts.

If you scored most of the items 3, 4, or 5, then more often than not, if not all the time, you perceive your spouse to be responsive to you. You believe your spouse will consider your perspective and respond in a considerate and caring way. If you scored any of the questions 2, 1, or 0, consider why, as that area of your relationship could be of concern.

We can give you an idea of what your score means on the entire Haven of Safety Scale. If you scored most of the items 3, 4, or 5, then more often than not, if not all the time, you perceive your spouse to be a safe haven. You trust that your spouse will be there for you and respond in a considerate and caring manner. If you scored most of the questions 2, 1, or 0, consider why, as you probably don't perceive your relationship to be a safe haven. Review which area you scored the lowest: trust, emotional availability, or responsiveness. Review why that area is of most concern.

Think over how your spouse would have answered the above questions. Review how you can change to make your relationship more of a safe haven. How can you be more trustworthy, more emotionally available, and more responsive?

Whether you are going through a season of conflict and disconnection, or if you are in a marriage you look forward to coming home to, we invite you to enter a season of renewal and growth. It is our prayer that even if your spouse is not in this growth process with you, *you* will risk growing in these areas so that you can be a witness to God's changing power in your life. This way your spouse will experience you as trustworthy, more emotionally available, and more responsive. Your willingness to grow as a person will bring you a sense of inner peace, and you will find yourself living a life that God blesses.

Chapter 4

WHAT CONNECTS YOUR HEARTS?

We are not equipped to face life alone, especially difficult aspects of life;
we are not equipped for it nor designed for it.

—SUSAN JOHNSON

Seemingly inseparable, the couple smiles radiantly, holds hands constantly, and kisses at every opportunity. Dreaming of a lifetime spent together, they see one another as the ideal mate. The idealization that accompanies romantic love casts a rosy glow across the whole world. This couple—Adam and Sue—epitomizes the magic of romance.

Do you recognize Adam and Sue? They represent every couple on their wedding day. On that blissful occasion, they are bound together by far more than nuptial vows. They are connected by a strong attraction to each other—to another person who is, in reality, someone each other barely knows—and by a superoptimistic hope that their love will last forever.

Now let's check in with them a year later. Adam and Sue are sharing an anniversary dinner. He has carefully remembered the flowers and card. She is wearing his favorite dress. But halfway through dinner, Adam says something that just doesn't sit right with Sue. He recalls the last time they were at that

47

restaurant. "Remember, Sue? You locked the keys in the car, and we spent the whole evening waiting for a locksmith!"

Sue feels this comment devalues her, with overtones that Adam loves her less than he used to. She suspects that she's a disappointment to him. In fact, in most of her relationships, Sue worries that she will be a disappointment and fears that others won't care for her as much as she cares for them. And so now she sits, vulnerable and hurt. It's sad, because all she really wants is for them to have a wonderful evening, and for Adam to take pleasure in her.

But because she's hurt, Sue reacts with anger and criticizes Adam. "You know, this is so typical of you. You always do the same thing. You can't just enjoy the evening. No, you have to bring up something I've done wrong. Well, I haven't forgotten—you've ruined many a night!"

Adam is taken aback. He had meant no malice. Vulnerable to feeling criticized and rejected by Sue, Adam experiences Sue's strong reaction as suffocating and overwhelming. He feels misunderstood and worthless . . . and justified in his caution about not getting too close. Since he has learned over the course of all his relationships that it is best to be independent, not to rely too much on someone else, he defends himself.

"Sue, you are so far from what I said! I should carry around a tape recorder because you always take what I say and just twist it. You know, the problem is that you and I see things so differently. We'll never agree. As far as I can see, it's just hopeless."

She yells back that he is incapable of having any deep emotion, an attack that only drives him farther away.

The sad result? Sue feels that Adam is insensitive about her feelings and doesn't really value her. And Adam feels frustrated and is more cautious than ever about putting his heart in Sue's hand. Both Adam and Sue are left protecting their hearts from being hurt and fighting to get the other to see their wrong, change, and then come close. But it never happens; they never quite connect. Instead, on what should have been a lovely evening, they struggle through dinner and drive home in silence.

What happened between the wedding day and the first anniversary? Both Sue and Adam longed for their marriage to be a safe haven, even if they couldn't articulate it. Both desired to be understood and valued by the other.

And what they wanted out of the marriage from the beginning hasn't really changed. Paradoxical as it may seem, like so many couples who crave a safe haven marriage, Adam and Sue began fighting hatefully in a misguided attempt to get the very love they long for. This is the case with most couples who fight.

Can we find a way to understand why Sue and Adam, for example, fight the way they do? What happened that enabled one seemingly innocent comment to turn their dream date into a nightmare? What triggered Sue's criticism? What caused Adam to defend himself? Why did they both feel angry and hurt? Why can't they ever seem to come close instead of fighting and pushing each other away?

To understand this, we need to have a clear understanding of relationships, how they work, what connects two people, and what goes on to shift husbands and wives who long for closeness into a mode of fighting and disconnecting. We think the attachment theory best describes marital relationships.

ATTACHING LIKE VELCRO

I (Arch) have several hobbies that involve sticking things together. I have an interest, therefore, in many bonding techniques—not just the glues used in woodworking and boatbuilding, but also in the arc and gas welding used in metalwork. But of all the bonding techniques that have been invented, Velcro fascinates me the most. It can connect powerfully or disconnect easily, and it never leaves a mess. Have you ever examined this remarkable bonding agent? I must admit that when it first came out, I couldn't put my magnifying glass down as I observed at close quarters how each side attached and detached. Such simplicity! Millions of tiny hooks on one side and a mesh of fibers on the other. The hooks penetrate the fibers, and the two sides bond together. Once attached, Velcro stays firmly in place and only detaches when firmly pulled apart.

This brings us to a fundamental concept around which safe haven marriages are built—namely, how emotional attachments are formed and maintained between people—and Velcro serves as a helpful analogy. We literally attach ourselves to significant people like some sort of emotional Velcro. Our hearts and lives intricately connect to those we deeply care for. The hooks and fibers of our hearts and lives intertwine and connect with the meshed fibers of our loved ones, and we emotionally bond.

The intensity of these attachments varies depending on the nature of the relationship. We connect more with some people than with others. The bond we have with our coworkers or acquaintances, for example, will differ from the bond we have with our close friends or siblings. Our strongest bonds are between parents and children, and husbands and wives. We experience the most intense emotions when we are making, maintaining, or breaking these bonds. The deepest human feelings accompany our closest relationships.

In this chapter we'll look a little closer at the hooks and fibers that connect you and your spouse. We will describe the relationship Velcro, or attachment system, which is an intricate biological system that keeps you and your spouse emotionally connected. And we will examine what happens when you feel as if the bond that connects you and your spouse is being pulled apart. We'll show you what is at the heart of marital conflict and demonstrate what really happens when couples fight.

THE IMPORTANCE OF BONDS

Research confirms the importance of human bonds: Without relationships we humans wither and die, both emotionally and physically. The quality of our life diminishes when there is no one to share it with—family, friends, or spouse. As we have already seen, we were created for relationships. Everything about us was designed to live in close community and interaction with others. We certainly were not designed to go through life emotionally disconnected. And when we marry, an important and lifelong bond is formed—the connection between us and our spouse.

MARITAL BONDS GROW OVER TIME

I (Arch) will never forget becoming a father. When our second child was conceived (our first was stillborn), I had rather strange, mixed feelings toward the unnamed baby as it developed in my wife's womb—feelings that I didn't really expect. After all, parenting is a scary business, and an unborn baby doesn't yet feel like a person you can know and love. This little stranger moved around a lot, kicked, and made its presence felt. But soon-to-be fathers are one step removed from any tactile contact, so we carry a mixed bag of feelings—or at least I did.

A mother, on the other hand, begins to feel some attachment to the baby almost from the outset, since it is an extension of her body. Like me, most young fathers feel scared of any feelings and are uncertain about what lies ahead.

But then it happened. The moment I saw our daughter, as if by magic, wonder sprang up inside me. All it took was some visual contact, and I was literally overwhelmed by a surge of attachment feelings. This was *my* child. She was a *real person* who could be touched and loved. Almost miraculously, in the blink of an eye, an instant bond was formed in my heart. We became emotionally attached with bonds that seemed unbreakable. This experience repeated itself with our next child, Sharon, and our third, Sylvia.

In contrast with this immediate bonding, the connection between a husband and wife is not instantaneous. It grows and deepens over time and through shared experiences. During your dating years, you and your spouse were sexually attracted to each other, and this attraction kept you connected. But once you were married, the bond grew beyond mere sexuality and the need for your relationship to be a safe haven became vitally important. It takes about two years for a safe haven bond to be fully formed. And, like the bond between you and your children, the bond between you and your spouse is designed to last a lifetime.

THE BIOLOGICAL NATURE OF RELATIONSHIPS

Interestingly, the process that regulates and guides our reactions and responses in relationships is biological or physiological. There is a specific link between your physiology and your relationships. Think about what it feels like when your spouse massages your back and whispers in your ear, "I love you." It warms you all over. When you are close to your spouse, you are soothed and comforted. Your heart rate slows down, your blood flow regulates, and your body releases hormones that help you relax. It's a memorable experience.

You also likely can remember what it felt like the last time you were angry at your spouse. Maybe you felt that your husband didn't care about you anymore. Maybe you thought your wife would never understand you. When you feared being abandoned, your autonomic nervous system kicked into high gear, causing your blood to flow faster, your heart to pound, your breathing to increase, and your palms to sweat.

All this happens when we are afraid of our bond being threatened. Relationships and their implications affect the chemical processes in our brains that regulate our emotions, our ability to deal with and bounce back from stressful situations, and our ability to heal and recover from illness. Without a doubt we are intricately connected and "fearfully and wonderfully made" (Psalm 139:14).

RELATIONSHIPS: THE INTRICATE ATTACHMENT SYSTEM

The emotional tie that connects two people in a significant relationship is called an "attachment bond." In the 1950s, relationship researcher John Bowlby came up with this term to describe the deep connection between a parent and a child. He later applied it to the relationship between husband and wife. Bowlby spent his life trying to understand the workings of relationships. He was focused on making sense out of how close relationships come to be the source of comfort and security, or of pain and distress. John Bowlby's attachment theory describes and helps explain the attachment bond, the connection between a husband and wife.

According to Bowlby, the attachment system is like a thermostat that regulates how close and connected we are to others. The marital relationship includes an intimate physical connection that ties a couple together in a deep way. It is a reciprocal relationship where both husband and wife are mutually giving and receiving love. Over time, a marriage becomes a safe haven to which we can turn for love and comfort, and a secure base from which we can venture out into the world. When we sense that our spouse is not there for us or that our connection with our spouse is threatened, we make attempts to restore the connection.

Our first bond is with our parents and other caregivers. We are born into the shelter of these relationships, and there we are nurtured and become the persons we are. These relationships teach us about our world around us, about ourselves, about others, and about what we can expect in our relationships. Early relationships shape our expectations about all our future relationships and inform us how to behave in them. And it is in relationships that we continue to grow, mature, and become all that God has for us!

THE RELATIONSHIP THERMOSTAT

John Bowlby likened the attachment system to a thermostat. The aim of the relationship thermostat is to keep the relationship at a comfortable, connected setting. The thermostat in your home is probably set at a comfortable temperature—not too hot and not too cold. When the house gets too warm or too cold, the thermostat kicks on the heater or the air conditioner until the designated comfortable temperature is reached once again.

This is very similar to what happens in our relationships. You and your spouse have a certain level of comfort that is set for the following:

- Closeness or intimacy
- Emotional availability and accessibility to each other
- Sensitive responsiveness to one another
- The sense that you are loved and valued by each other

The attachment system is designed to keep you and your spouse close and connected and to regulate uncomfortable distance or closeness. When we marry, we establish what seems to be a comfortable relationship temperature. What is comfortable closeness, or the right amount of attentiveness and sensitive responsiveness? Your attachment system alerts you when your spouse is not close enough, not available or responsive enough. When you sense that your spouse is not there for you, your attachment system, like the thermostat, clicks on to restore a comfortable connection between you and your spouse. This system is innate and is a necessary element in all relationships.

THE BEHAVIORAL ATTACHMENT SYSTEM

Have you ever put your hand too close to the flame on your gas stove? Remember what happened? You pulled your hand away as fast as you could! This is the wonderful design of your autonomic nervous system.

Deep within our brains we have reflexive neural pathways that help us react to emotional danger or pain within our relationships. This system guides how we act, react, feel, and heal in relationships. When you sense that your loved one doesn't value or love you, or is physically or emotionally disconnected from you, emotions and behaviors are instantly triggered that try to recover the loss of this closeness.

This system—which we call the attachment system—is a set of emotions and behaviors that seek to restore closeness and to obtain your spouse's understanding and responsiveness. The attachment system is designed to do three things:

1. To protest emotional disconnection
2. To get your loved one to see that you are disconnected
3. To get your loved one to respond in a caring manner

You see this clearly when children stretch out their arms and smile in an effort to be picked up, or when they cry and protest being put down when Mom has to start supper. You also see it when a child screams and races up and down the aisles when lost at the grocery store. The child is trying to say, "Hey, I don't like being separated from you! I want to find you so I can be close to you again." These behaviors are efforts to protest against disconnection, to get the attention of a loved one, and to get her to respond in a caring manner.

If a parent is attuned to a child, she is able to tell what the cries of the child mean. You hear a mom say, "Oh, Dustin is crying—he's wet" or, "Sadie is screaming—she's hungry." The cries of the child are a protest against what they are feeling: "I feel wet, cold, and achy in my tummy, and I don't like it." The cries are also an effort to obtain the attention of the parent: "Do you notice that I am uncomfortable? Can I get your attention over here?" And to get the parent to respond: "Come and feed me."

The attachment system includes nonverbal expressions, verbal expressions, and particular behaviors. The nonverbals include smiles and warm, concerned, or empathetic looks. They also include those "dirty looks" that let you know your spouse is mad at you and you are in trouble. You may also see frowns, pursed lips, cold stares, blank expressions, the shaking of the head, or folded arms.

Verbal expressions include crying, asking, talking, sharing openly and thoughtfully, apologizing, forgiving, reconnecting, and sharing your concern. Couples who sense that they can't get their spouse's attention by talking may display more aggressive responses like criticizing, screaming, nagging, fighting, arguing, defensiveness, blaming, withdrawing, or shutting down. The experiences in our early relationships shape how we react to being hurt and how we reach out for comfort and support in our marriages.

If your experiences with your parents and earlier relationships confirmed that people are accessible and that you can reach them with ease, you will use tactics such as asking, sharing your thoughts, crying, expressing sadness, talking, and otherwise communicating. But if you feel that despite your efforts, no one will respond to you with care and concern, you may feel like screaming. Or you may begin to shut down the desire for comfort from others. You begin to feel that being independent is actually strength.

These attachment behaviors are often automatic responses, done without thinking. Suppose, for instance, that your husband comes home late from work on your date night, and you have been looking forward all day to being close to him. He walks in the door and you yell at him for his inconsideration—he didn't call to tell you he would be late.

From the husband's point of view, his wife is yelling at him for being late and inconsiderate, when he, too, was looking forward to being with her all day and was just as frustrated as she, sitting in gridlock traffic, trying to get home. But now, as he hears her angry words, he defends himself and then shuts her out. All this takes place without thought. Both spouses responded unconsciously, reacting instantly because of the hurt, disappointment, or anger they felt.

Of course, sometimes we are well aware of how we're reacting. Andrea recalls being so upset at dinner with her husband that she intentionally knocked over a glass of water on the table at the restaurant.

"I was so hurt by what he'd said," she explained. "No matter how I tried to get him to understand how hurt I felt, he just kept telling me how I was just making a big deal out of nothing. I so much wanted him to notice how he had hurt me. So I knocked over the glass of water. I was trying to tell him, 'Just understand my hurt and come close.'"

All these behaviors are possible when our connection with someone we love is interrupted. Fears of being abandoned or found unlovable are fundamental human fears. They are so basic and so profound that they can trigger very severe reactions in our nervous systems. Sometimes they may even cause some major depressive responses and panic attacks.

How does our attachment system respond? With panic, clinging, crying, anger, pouting, defending, arguing, criticizing, pulling away, shutting down, and, last but not least, falling silent. Do any of those responses sound familiar to you? What kinds of events can cause such reactions? We may react when we sense any of the following:

- You didn't call me, and when you did your voice sounded distant.
- You didn't stop to listen to how I was feeling.
- I was lost and couldn't find you.
- I was afraid you might be mad or disappointed in me.
- I sensed you were too busy for me.
- I sensed you were disappointed in me.
- I felt I was losing control.
- I felt you would not take care of me.
- I didn't trust you had my best interest at heart.
- You were blaming me.
- You think less of me.
- I thought you didn't trust me with the responsibility.
- You didn't do what I wanted even though you knew how important it was to me.

ATTACHMENT STYLES OR DIFFERENT WAYS OF CONNECTING

In order to understand your marriage better, and so help strengthen the attachment between you and your spouse, let's first look at some past attachments and see how they may be affecting the present. We'll use four fictional children to illustrate four different ways of responding to the emotional availability and responsiveness of the people in our lives. First, we will take a look at the attachments between Johnny and his parents, and then those of three other children and their parents.

Johnny and His Parents: The Confident Connection

Playing in the park, four-year-old Johnny is king of the junglegym. Glancing over at his dad and mom, who are sitting on a bench, talking and caring for his baby sister, Johnny plays with confidence. Occasionally he becomes concerned because he is climbing too high and fears that he might fall. At that point, Johnny stops in the midst of his play to look over to Dad and Mom for assurance. With this look he is asking, "Am I too high? Can I handle this? Am I still safe? Are Mom and Dad still close?"

Dad and Mom glance back at Johnny, smile, wave, and sometimes shout words of encouragement. "That looks like fun, Johnny!" They are, in both word and action, reassuring Johnny that they are there, that he is capable of climbing, that he is safe, and that the world is his to explore. This confidence building enables Johnny to continue in his adventures.

Then a stranger walks into the sand pit. Johnny feels afraid. He falls off the junglegym. Feeling some pain in his knee, Johnny begins to cry and runs toward his parents. He climbs into his mother's lap and nestles his head against her. Mom holds Johnny, rocks him, and strokes his head. Dad checks his knee. No major damage. Johnny soaks up the comfort and reassurance. Before long, he lifts his head, looks around, and crawls out of his mother's lap. "Dad, watch how high I can swing!" And off he goes, once again secure that he can conquer the world.

Now glance over to the other side of the park, where three other children are at play. Let's see how these children interact with their parents.

Joey and His Parents: The Guarded Connection

Joey, also four, is on the junglegym too, but when he feels he has climbed too high, is hurt, or is afraid because a stranger is present, he does not look up at his parents for assurance. He has learned over time that his parents will reject his cries for comfort. They will either be too busy talking, or they will scold him for being scared, saying, "Joey, big boys don't cry! Stop that crying!"

If he were to run over to his parents in pain, they would respond insensitively to his cries. "Stand up straight," they would demand, "and don't lean all over me. Stop being a baby and go play." Joey's mother sees her son's crying as manipulation; Joey's dad sees it as immaturity—Joey is "being a baby." So Joey has learned not to show his distress, although he feels it inside. He reaches for his toys and comforts himself or becomes distracted by another activity.

Jackie and Her Parents: The Concerned Connection

Five-year-old Jackie is playing in the sandbox, and when she is scared, wants to show off the sandcastle she made, or gets sand in her eyes, she runs to her parents. Her parents are, on the surface, warm and caring. But whenever Jackie gets upset or displays emotion, her parents became frustrated. Thus they are less than attentive and responsive to Jackie.

Because they are not attuned to Jackie's needs, they aren't quite sure what Jackie wants and are unable to soothe her. "What's wrong?" they ask uncertainly. "I can't understand you when you're crying."

Jackie also feels unsure—unsure whether her parents are able to support her and be a source of comfort to her. Therefore she ratchets her attempts to get her parents' attention up a notch. She mixes her longing to be soothed by her parents with the anger and frustration of not being soothed. Sometimes she sits in the sandbox and screams at the top of her voice, throwing her toys and crying. That's the only way she knows to get her parents' attention. Once they are listening, she runs to them and throws herself into their laps. Even then, however, she continues to cry and is not really comforted.

Jennifer and Her Parents: The Cautious Connection

Jennifer, who is five too, is also on the junglegym. Sometimes when she feels hurt or afraid, she seeks out her parents. At other times she acts in what seem like strange ways, in a very disorganized manner. Sometimes she walks toward her parents, then suddenly turns around and walks backward to them. Other times she cries and yells, running toward her mother then suddenly stopping and falling to the floor in a tantrum. Jennifer's parents try to go to her and comfort her, but she deliberately falls to the floor again as they approach her.

Jennifer's parents, meanwhile, are very inconsistent in how they comfort her. Sometimes they are responsive, even intrusive and overwhelming to Jennifer. At other times they are punishing, distant, and cold. Frustrated when they can't soothe Jennifer, they scold her severely. Jennifer never knows if she is a bad little girl or "Mommy's precious angel."

Interesting children. But maybe you're wondering how their behavior and their parents' responses relate to our goal of safe haven marriage. As you'll soon see, they relate very much indeed. Childhood relationships serve as a lens that colors the way we see others when we grow up. And we bring this into our marriage relationship. These stories illustrate the key components of an attachment bond.

THE IMPACT OF OUR EARLY RELATIONSHIPS

Children learn early on whether or not their parents will be there when they reach for them. The responses of their parents communicate to them how lovable they are, how lovable others are, and how safe the world is.

Early interactions between children and their parents literally create neural pathways for how they will, as adults, deal with their emotions, express their needs, regulate their stress, deal with difficult situations, and soothe themselves. These interactions, expectations, beliefs, and values regarding relationships are internalized and taken into marital relationships. Depending upon the emotional availability and responsiveness of your spouse, your marital relationship will either confirm or correct your earlier relationship experiences.

THE COMPONENTS OF ATTACHMENT

There are three key components that bond us to one another: *close proximity, haven of safety,* and a *secure base.* When any of these are disrupted or threatened, the relationship thermostat clicks on and the attachment system is triggered.

Let's review these components.

Close Proximity

Attachment bonds are formed when we are in close proximity to significant others. Generally, the more we spend time with someone, the more familiar and connected we become. As we've seen, the force that draws spouses together is usually sexual attraction. This keeps young couples together until a more enduring attachment bond develops. Sadly, some marriages never develop a deeper bond once the initial sexual attraction wears off.

But if a marriage survives the early stage, the attachment system functions to *keep* husbands and wives close and connected, creating a desire "just to be together." The desire to be close to your spouse, apart from sex, is not a sign of clinginess or weakness. It is a natural part of being human and being bonded. The touch, hold, or even mere presence of a caring spouse can soothe anxieties, slow the heart, calm breathing, and create a sense of tranquillity. It has the potential to help us manage our emotions and our stress, and to deal with life's difficulties.

Haven of Safety

The relationship between Johnny and his parents was a safe haven to which he could turn, knowing that his parents would be emotionally available and responsive to him. His parents were available to Johnny when he needed them, and they responded to him with care and concern. They neither smothered Johnny when he needed to venture off nor ignored Johnny when he needed closeness and comfort.

How does this tie in to marriage? We all need the safe arms of our spouse to turn to for care and encouragement. Think back to the story of Adam and Sue at the beginning of this chapter. In the early stages of their love, sexual desire and idealization held them together. But over time, this passionate form of love must mature into genuine intimacy. The degree to which spouses are able—like Johnny's parents—to be a source of comfort and strength becomes increasingly important over time.

The greatest predictor of marital satisfaction and longevity is the presence of *trust, emotional availability,* and *sensitive responsiveness.* This determines whether you perceive your relationship to be a safe haven.

After one year of dating and one year of marriage, Adam and Sue were just beginning to transition to a more mature relationship. They were learning how to be attuned to each other's needs and sensitive to each other's vulnerable places. Each was discovering how to be emotionally available and responsive, encouraging individual growth while being close and a constant source of comfort.

Building a safe haven is a process born in close proximity, often as a result of conflict and time spent together. Conflict is often a way you and your spouse discover the truth about each other and come to terms with your differences. But once you work through the conflicts and difficulties, what lies ahead can literally become a heaven on earth—and I (Arch) am speaking from personal experience, having been married for forty-seven years.

Secure Base

What does this stage accomplish? Ultimately, it means you have constructed a secure base from which a husband or wife can confidently venture into the world. When this base is established, you'll have the courage and freedom to explore life, knowing you can always return to a place of security where you are loved, supported, and nurtured. Independence naturally develops when you are securely attached. You can't launch out into life until you know you have a safe haven and a secure base, whether you are in kindergarten, going away to college, or venturing through life with your spouse.

As we return to the experiences of the children at the park, we see how each child learned to use or not to use their parents as a secure base from which to venture out into the world. Just as Johnny's parents encouraged their son that he was quite able to face the difficulties of the junglegym, so do we instill in our spouse a sense that they can face whatever life brings. Your responses to your husband can help him develop a deep assurance that he is able to succeed and give your spouse courage to face whatever lies ahead. You can respect and encourage your wife's development as a person and her desire to grab life with both hands. As Johnny's parents were able to assess what he needed and provide a balance of nurturing and independence, so your sensitivity toward your spouse encourages closeness while allowing your spouse to grow as a person. More significantly, because of his parents' well-balanced approach, at the core of his being Johnny felt loved and believed himself to be lovable. And in your marriage, depending upon how you and your spouse interrelate, you are left with a deep sense that you are capable, lovable, and able to go through life victoriously.

AM I LOVABLE? ARE YOU SAFE?

Our early relationships determine how lovable or unlovable we feel. If our caregivers were trustworthy, emotionally available, and responsive to us, then we will have developed a sense that we are worthy of being loved. If our parents were cold when we approached them for understanding, distant when we needed warmth, or absent when we needed a cheerleader, we came to believe that even though we longed for closeness, others close to us had the potential to hurt and disappoint. Our heart was not safe in their hands.

From childhood on, we continue to evaluate whether a particular person is a "safe" person, able to love us and care for us, willing to be there for us if we reach for him. We evaluate whether that person will be loving, caring, and emotionally trustworthy. And we also continue to evaluate ourselves. Particularly as we pass through emotional challenges, we ask ourselves two questions. First, we ask, "Am I lovable? Am I the type of person others can enjoy and love?"

Next we ask, "Is this other person willing and able to love me? Is he the sort of person who will love me? Will she be accessible, caring, and willing to be there for me when I reach for her?"

THE ANSWER IS EITHER YES OR NO

There are four possible combinations when answering these questions, and the four children we met earlier will help us understand them and discover how they impact a marital relationship.

I am lovable, and others are lovable and able to love me.

Johnny's parents demonstrated sensitive and caring reactions to his needs and failings, which reflected to Johnny that he was lovable. He was assured that he was able to get the love and comfort that he needed.

His parents' trustworthiness, emotional availability, and sensitive responsiveness toward Johnny also assured him that others could be trusted to give him love and comfort. He did not doubt that his parents would respond to him when he needed them. In this way, he was assured of two things: that he is lovable, and that the world is a safe place in which others are able and willing to love him.

I am lovable, but others are not willing or able to love me.

Joey, as we've discovered, had a different experience with his parents. His mother and father were aware of him and his needs, but they were not encouraging to him when he cried out for help. Those with more guarded parental connections such as Joey's may view themselves as lovable, worthy people. However, because of past experiences, people like Joey view others as unable to love them the way they need to be loved.

Others are willing and able to love me, but they don't because I am not a lovable person.

Jackie did not feel heard, and she could not figure out how to get the attention of her parents when she needed them. She cried and screamed, and even after her parents finally paid attention to her, she never really felt comforted. As an adult, Jackie will probably view herself as unlovable. She may believe that her spouse is a loving person, worthy of her love, and she will be there for them. But she may also think that, due to her own unworthiness, her husband is unwilling or unable to love her. In her eyes others are lovable; she is unlovable.

I am not lovable, and others are neither willing nor able to love me.

Those like Jennifer, who have an unclear or "cautious" relationship with their parents, are never on solid ground in their relationships. They don't know what to expect; they see others as untrustworthy, unavailable, and unresponsive—in a word, unlovable. They also see themselves as unlovable.

Remember Adam and Sue? Sue came to the marriage with a sense that she was not very lovable. She sensed that others would be able to love her if she would only do more to please them, if she would simply change and be different. She viewed Adam as able to give her the love she needed, but because of her own failings, he was unwilling to. She fears that she was a big disappointment to him, and that Adam will one day find out that she is an unworthy woman and will leave her.

INTERNAL WORKING MODELS

Our adult emotional reactions and overreactions don't suddenly spring up out of a vacuum. They are rooted in our early history—the way we felt in our early relationships was internalized; our responses to those feelings became our internal working models. These are beliefs, expectations, and feelings about ourselves and others. They are like internal sunglasses that color how we view our relationships. We bring into our marriages our internal working models, our ways of being in relationship. And we have preconceived ideas and expectations as to how our spouse will respond to them.

For example, Sue's basic assumption about others is that they are capable of providing love and support, but because of her failings they are unwilling to do so. And the only way to get others' attention and to get them to respond to her needs is by getting angry and yelling.

On the other hand, Adam has come to assume that relying on others is useless. They will only disappoint him and tell him to take care of himself, anyway. He has become self-reliant and capable of comforting himself. He is therefore able to shut Sue out and find satisfaction in his work.

The more Sue tries to obtain Adam's attention by yelling angrily, the more Adam confirms his assumption that relationships are overwhelming. He feels hurt, so he also feels justified in being self-reliant and withdrawing. But the more Sue senses that Adam is moving away from her, the more she is convinced that people are untrustworthy, unavailable, and unresponsive. This makes her angrier than ever, and she yells even louder.

As we will see in future chapters, this attempt to regulate closeness and be seen as worthy sets in motion interactional cycles that keep couples disconnected.

NEW EXPERIENCES

Over the course of your life, these internal working models are revised and changed according to your experiences with those closest to you. For example, if you experienced your parents as absent, not involved in your life, then that experience is internalized. You come to believe that people will not be there for you, and so you become self-sufficient in order to cope. But over the course of your relationships and marriage, you have new experiences with your loved ones. Your best friend is there for you, and your spouse is there for you. And in seeking a relationship with God, you come to find that God can also be there for you.

This new experience changes everything. It changes how you view yourself: as someone who is worthy of being loved. And changes how you view others: as people who can be trusted to care for you and love you. This change enables you to reach for your spouse in a new and different way. You are able to give your heart to your spouse with confidence that you are worthy of love. Your spouse will be both able and willing to love you in return. The purpose of this book is to help bring about such change. In that way you can foster a marriage you can come home to.

SUMMING UP

Your attachment system is a marvelous mix of emotions, behaviors, and beliefs, all programmed into your brain to help you stay in relationship with those you have bonded with. In marriage, this attachment system is natural and purposefully designed to keep husband and wife emotionally and physically connected. But, as we will see, cycles of conflict often hinder couples from being able to meet each other's attachment needs. Whenever your attachment to your spouse is threatened, attachment behaviors are triggered in an attempt to get the attention of your spouse, in order to recover your emotional and physical connection.

It bears repeating: You and your spouse may have developed bad patterns of relating including yelling, nagging, and fighting, but that doesn't mean all is lost. Emotional outbursts are often a desperate cry of your soul for your partner to reach out and restore your heart to its rightful place of safety. In the next chapter, we'll take a closer look at attachment styles, and how you and your spouse can put them to work in your marriage to create the safe haven marriage you so deeply desire.

REFLECTION QUESTIONS

1. Draw a time line of your life. At each stage of your life, who was there for you? Who did you turn to for comfort and care when you were happy or sad?

2. How did your parents respond to you when you were hurt, happy, or needed them? How did their response affect your life?

3. Over the years, how have other relationships shaped your life?

4. How have these patterns/ways of relating impacted your marriage?

Chapter 5

HOW DO YOUR HEARTS CONNECT?

We are all happiest and able to use our talents to their best when we are confident that standing behind us are trusted people who will be there should difficulties arise.

—JOHN BOWLBY

Swords in hand, the four princes galloped toward the castle. Seeing the four princesses eagerly leaning out of the castle tower window, they signaled that the drawbridge be lowered. "My prince!" each princess whispered. "My prince has come to love me and claim my love."

The first princess ran from the window with great anticipation, through the corridors of the castle and down to the gate where she could welcome her prince with open arms. She had waited a long time for his return, and deep in her heart she was assured that his return was trustworthy. He had promised to love her all his life. She had no reason not to believe him now. They would live happily ever after.

The three remaining princesses also darted joyfully from the window. But then they stopped, uncertain of what they might discover. Slowly they turned and made their way back to the tower window overlooking the castle gate. There they leaned forward, their eyes straining for a better view of their princes as they came nearer, looking for any sign that would reassure them of their princes' unwavering love. *Is that my prince come to love me, or a dragon masquerading as a prince?* each wondered.

As they drew near to the castle, the galloping princes pulled back on their reins, the horses skidding to a halt.

What is that? they each wondered, seeing the faces at the castle tower window. *My princess whom I long to love, or a dragon dressed up as a princess waiting to devour me?*

AM I LOVABLE?

From early in our lives until the day we die, we ask our loved ones, "Can I trust you to be emotionally available, accessible, and responsive when I need you?"[1] Our parents were our earliest mirrors, reflecting back to us our worth and meaning. Then came family and other relationships across our life span. If our loved ones were emotionally available and responsive, we will feel cared for and secure in all our relationships. We'll feel that those close to us can be trusted to give us the love we need. We'll also be comfortable with closeness and secure enough to express our hurts and needs in ways that draw us together.

Not having someone who was a good, truthful mirror early in life can severely damage the way we love in later relationships. "Am I lovable? Will you value me?" When parents and loved ones are silent or punishing, their answers are interpreted as, "You are only loved if you fulfill my expectations . . . I doubt whether you are valuable . . . no, you are probably not valuable or lovable." We dim the light in our hearts and our attitude becomes, "I don't care if you see me as worthless. I will just keep to myself and never trust anyone to love me."

Closeness doesn't come easily when for years you have received uncertain love messages. Intimacy is regulated. You look for various ways of getting your love needs met; you seek for someone to understand and love you. Often, the ways you try to do that are defensive ways. Even after you feel you've found a life partner, you come to marriage with preset beliefs and expectations, values, and feelings pertaining to the following crucial issues:

- Expectations of what real intimacy feels and looks like
- Ways of responding to hurt, disconnection, or disappointment

- A sense of being unlovable or unworthy, questioning whether you are able to obtain easily and comfortably the love you need from others
- A sense of the emotional safety or unsafety of others; questioning whether others can be trusted to love and take care of your heart

These have all been shaped by your early life experiences. How your parents emotionally cared for you is mixed in with the behavior of others in close relationships, with your personality, and with the culture that surrounds you. This mix becomes an internalized road map that determines the way you view yourself and others, and how you process and respond in intimate relationships. The way you perceive what goes on in your relationships and how you respond is your attachment style, which we introduced in the previous chapter. An attachment style is a way of being in a relationship.

As we saw in the illustration featuring our four princes and four princesses, at the beginning of the chapter, you come to your marital relationship with either an assurance that your prince or princess is what he or she is supposed to be, or you are convinced that your spouse is potentially unsafe and unable to love you, incapable of being emotionally available and responsive to you.

ATTACHMENT STYLES

In the previous chapter, we outlined the purpose of the attachment system. The attachment emotional and behavioral system is triggered when you feel that your attachment bond is being threatened. You sense that your spouse is not close, emotionally available, or responsive. You feel unseen, misunderstood, and unvalued. So the attachment system triggers emotions and behaviors such as fear, sadness, anger, pursuit, clinging, silence, or withdrawing. The reactions to being hurt serve the following purposes:

- To let your spouse know that he or she has hurt you
- To get your spouse to recognize his or her wrong for having done so
- To get your spouse to move close and be emotionally accessible and responsive

Four attachment styles have been identified, and a proper understanding of them is essential to building a safe haven marriage: *secure, anxious, avoidant,* and *fearful* (which, in children, is identified as disorganized/ambivalent).[2]

We laid the foundation for understanding attachment styles in the previous chapter. Now let's look at these four attachment styles to see how they impact your marriage relationship, particularly how they affect your need for comfort and care. An understanding of these styles will also illumine why and how you and your spouse fight. A detailed explanation of these attachment styles is shown below.

THE FOUR ATTACHMENT STYLES: WAYS OF BEING IN CLOSE RELATIONSHIP[3]

1. SECURE	*2. ANXIOUS*
connected with certainty	*connected with uncertainty*
Comfortable with closeness	Preoccupied with relationships
Don't fear abandonment	Desire closeness, worry about its absence
View self as lovable	Feel insecure and not always lovable
"Others are willing and able to care for my heart."	"Others are able to be there, but might abandon me because of my faults."
Understanding of and appropriate expression of emotions	Emotional roller coaster—feel close and safe—then angry, sad, and clingy
No anxiety about abandonment	High anxiety about being abandoned or receiving insufficient love
Self is lovable	Self is unlovable
3. AVOIDANT	*4. FEARFUL*
connected carefully	*connected cautiously*
Uncomfortable with closeness	Fearful of closeness

Self-sufficient, doesn't fear abandonment	Anxious about being abandoned
Feel worthy of love	Fear they are not worthy of love
"Others may not be willing or able to give me what I need—but that's okay, I don't need closeness anyway."	"Others are untrustworthy, hurtful, and unable to love me."
Avoids certain emotions that'll trigger attachment system; makes less of or dismisses other emotions	Emotions are scary and overwhelming.

SECURE ATTACHMENT STYLE: CONNECTED WITH CERTAINTY

What does a securely attached couple look like? It can be summed up with the following statement: "I know you will be there for me." Take Brad and Trisha, for example. They are far from perfect, but they have some unique qualities that make their relationship a safe haven.

Brad and Trisha are able to turn to each other when they are troubled or need comfort. They both have an inner assurance that they are lovable and valued. Brad knows that Trish will be emotionally available when he needs her, and Trish knows this of Brad.

Like Brad and Trisha, when both partners have a secure attachment style, spouses are able to seek comfort from their partners in nondefensive and nondestructive ways. They don't fear that their spouse will leave or not love them enough. So they don't feel the need to criticize, cling, cry, or coerce their spouse into being accessible and responsive. Jealousy is also absent. And if they do have some fear about whether their spouse will be accessible or responsive, they are able to openly and honestly discuss this with their spouse and resolve their fears.

These couples are comfortable with closeness, so they don't need to avoid intimate emotions or shy away from issues surrounding intimacy. They are not crushed or devastated if their spouse feels some disappointment, so they don't turn every disagreement into a catastrophe. They are able to receive input from and be influenced by their spouse. And in this way, their arguments are resolved quickly. Somehow through their conflict, their relationship is strengthened.

There is one very significant feature about the attachment of two secure people: *Secure couples still fight.*

Brad and Trisha know what starts their fights. So when there is a disagreement or conflict, they quickly steer it away from destructiveness and toward a productive outcome. They are able to express their hurt, disappointment, and even anger directly and openly—because they are comfortable with their feelings and can constructively communicate them without fear of rejection. Their anger is used to bring about valid and constructive change. And in the end, their fights leave them more connected than before, with a deeper understanding of one another.

Now let's make one point very clear: The relationship between two secure people is never a perfect one. It is unrealistic to expect this of any relationship. Ups and downs are inevitable. Let's observe Brad and Trisha as they tell us about how they dealt with a recent fight. See if you can pick up some ideas about what makes their relationship a secure bond. I highlight in italics what makes their statement or interaction descriptive of a secure attachment bond.

"Like just the other night," Trisha begins. "Brad, with his sarcastic sense of humor, made some smart-aleck remark that just hit me the wrong way. I know he really didn't mean harm by it, but it just hit my soft spot and it hurt."

Brad looks at Trisha and, laughing at himself, shakes his head. "Oh, yeah, I remember that, oh my gosh." Now they both laugh and smile at each other. *(There seems to be no built-up resentment from past fights lingering in their current interactions. Although Trisha was hurt by Brad's comment, she knows that in the bigger picture of their relationship, Brad is not out to hurt her intentionally.)*

"Yes," Brad recalls, "I said something I thought was innocent enough, but it hurt her."

"Something inside of me got hot and angry," Trish interjects. "So I pulled my hand out from under Brad's and got up from the couch." *(Securely attached people have feelings, often of anger, hurt, frustration, sadness, and disap-*

pointment—*the full spectrum. But they are able to manage these emotions. They recognize them quickly and take responsibility for their reactions, instead of attacking their spouse, saying, "Well, I wouldn't have reacted that way if he wasn't so insensitive. What am I supposed to do when he acts like a jerk to me?")*

"I knew I had said something insensitive the second it came out of my mouth," Brad admitted. "So I went up to her and asked her what the matter was. At first she said 'nothing.' But I knew she was hurt by what I had said." *(Brad was able to admit his part without defensiveness. That is, he didn't feel the need to retaliate with, "She takes everything too personally; it wasn't that big of a deal." Rather, he was able to take responsibility for what he said and accepted its impact on Trisha.)*

"I was hurt. I really wanted to talk about it at that point, but something inside of me just couldn't. Instead, I wanted to pull away. I just couldn't sit down and start sharing my feelings, because the feelings I had were hurt and anger. So I pulled away; shut down. I know it doesn't help anything when I do," confessed Trisha. *(Trisha is able to recognize her overreaction and move toward becoming more forthcoming in expressing her feelings. Securely attached people are far from being perfect—but they quickly accept and own their imperfections.)*

"So I came up to her and asked her again if she would tell me what hurt her because I didn't mean to hurt her." *(Instead of defending himself or withdrawing, Brad is able to come closer to Trisha and offer comfort and reconciliation.)*

"Well, I knew I didn't want to stay mad all night, and since we would eventually talk about what happened and resolve it anyway, I decided to sit next to him and start talking." *(Trisha has had past experiences with Brad where she has felt vulnerable and he responded with kindness and considerateness. She feels assured of Brad's consistent acceptance of her and her emotions.)*

"She didn't want me to hold her hand or sit too close, and that was okay. I know she needs a little bit of space when she is mad. So I sat on the other side of the couch and we talked." *(Brad respects Trisha's need for space as she sorts out her emotions, and he doesn't see this as a personal rejection.)*

"Yes, I just have to cool down before I can start talking. When we did, I told him that his joking sometimes crosses a line and hurts me. And his making fun of my cookies was not necessary. It was hurtful. I had spent all day juggling the kids and was still able to make a good meal with dessert. Even though the cookies were as hard as rocks, it hurt when he said, 'They'll be good as hockey pucks.'" *(Trisha is comfortable expressing her hurt and anger with Brad. From past experiences, she has a deep assurance that Brad will listen, consider her perspective, and respond positively to her vulnerability.)*

Brad turns to Trisha and once again expresses his heart. "I know. I was just trying to be cute. You looked so disappointed, and I just wanted to make you laugh. But I am sorry, Trisha. You are a good cook, and I appreciate all you do at home." *(Brad is able to admit to his part and move toward enriching the relationship. He is assured that Trisha will trust his good intentions.)*

And she does. Trisha turns to Brad and laughs good-humoredly. "Well, you know, I appreciate your apology. Thanks for seeing how that hurt me. You are right, though—those oatmeal cookies were as hard as rocks."

QUALITIES OF A SECURE ATTACHMENT

So what, then, are differences between securely attached couples and the other attachment styles? Securely attached couples are able to:

- Hold on to a deep sense that they are loved and valuable
- Know from experience that their spouse is trustworthy and will be loving, supportive, and responsive
- Understand, make sense of, and express their emotions appropriately
- Share their needs and hurts and reach out for others
- Make sense out of fights and get back on track when the fight is over
- Emotionally connect during and after fights

In a little more detail, here are the most significant features of securely attached couples:

Feel Sense of Value and Self-Worth

Over time securely attached people become instilled with a sense of value and self-worth. They feel secure and see other people as emotionally safe.

They readily accept that others will respond to them with love. From this solid place they are able to interact with others in an honest and certain way. They know that if they express their hurts, anger, or needs, their spouse will respond with understanding, comfort, and support.

Because of this security, Trisha knows that all she has to do is reach out for Brad, and he will respond. She only has to say, "Hey, when you get a minute tonight, I need to talk to you about something." She doesn't have to manipulate, test the water, or walk on eggshells trying to find just the right timing or words to get Brad's attention. She can be open, forthright, and honest.

Believe Spouse's Intentions Are Good

Securely attached people also believe that the intentions of their spouse are good. They are certain that their spouse has their best interest at heart. Like when Brad came through the back door one day, leaving the screen door open. Trisha yelled at him, "I can't believe you! How many times have I asked you to close the door behind you!" Brad could have taken Trisha's yelling personally. Defensively he could have yelled back, "Hey, do it yourself. Are you lame or something?" Or, "Ask the kids to do it; you never have them take any responsibility around here."

Instead, Brad quickly sizes up the situation, apologizes, and closes the door, attributing Trisha's outburst to her general frustration with flies, the noisy kids running in and out all day, and the nonfunctional air conditioner that is awaiting the repairman's attention. She is facing more than enough to make anyone short-fused. So Brad quickly forgets the incident. He doesn't store it in his resentment bank.

If Brad had felt that Trisha's yelling was uncalled for, he would have been confident enough to go to Trisha and say, "Hey, why all the yelling? I don't appreciate your yelling at me from across the house like that. Can we fix this?" Trisha would respect Brad's response and the impact of her yelling at him as a legitimate gripe, and in a short time they would have come to an understanding, regained control of their emotions, and restored their relationship.

Accept Each Other's Perspective

Securely attached couples are also able to accept each other's perspective. "We each have our own window through which we look at a situation. My view is often different from Brad's view," Trisha notes.

"But just because we have a different perspective doesn't mean that one of our perspectives is wrong and the other is right," adds Brad.

"That's right." Trisha nods. "Our windows are just different—two different outlooks on the world. Knowing this helps me try to understand why Brad feels the way he does. When I move to his window and look at the situation from his viewpoint, I quickly come to understand his perspective." Trisha realizes that Brad is not being thoughtless or insensitive; he just has a different viewpoint.

"I know I also have to move over to her window periodically and force myself to see the situation from her perspective. I may not agree with her perspective, but I have to understand it. Only then can we move toward a mutual window—one that we can both look out of."

View Spouse's Emotions As Valid

Securely attached couples are also able to accept that the emotions of their spouse are as valid as their own. They are able to realize that their spouse's wounded or angry feelings are for a good reason. And they are able to try to understand those reasons without being defensive, critical, or withdrawing. They are able to regulate their own emotions and expression of them. We will talk further about emotions in chapter 7.

Recover Quickly After Fights

Secure couples quickly get back on track after fights. Slamming the kitchen door, Trisha storms down the hallway and up the stairs toward her bedroom—her sanctuary. She wants to get away from the man she thought was charming and wonderful only ten minutes ago. Halfway up the stairs she pauses, reflecting on what just happened. Then she turns around and retraces her steps down the stairs and through the kitchen door. Once again she is standing in front of her husband.

"Brad," Trisha says, this time in a softer, gentler voice, "I don't want to criticize you or be angry at you. But I was just so hurt by what you did. I don't want to storm off. I would like to resolve this now. And if we can't see eye to eye, then that is not the end of our relationship. I guess we'll deal with it."

Brad opens his arms and motions for her to come rest her head against his chest. "I care for you so much. We don't have to solve this all tonight, you know. I am not going anywhere. Let's sit and regroup. Want a cup of coffee?"

Securely attached couples are quickly able to find their way back together during and after fights. Their arguments often turn into opportunities to understand each other in a deeper way, strengthening their bond.

ANXIOUS ATTACHMENT STYLE: CONNECTED WITH UNCERTAINTY

Do you love me? Do you really care about me? Will I always be one step away from really being loved by you? These are the questions uppermost in the minds of the next attachment style we will discuss, the anxious style.

Anxious couples have learned from early childhood that their connection with their parents may be lost, so they do all they can to stay as close as possible. They became people-pleasers, performers, caretakers, silent observers, and even angry pursuers, all in hopes of avoiding being unloved. They can become controlling in order to assure closeness. But it doesn't always work. Their clinging, crying, performing, and placating as a child didn't always ensure their parents' consistent love. And the attention doesn't always soothe their aching hearts.

Anxious spouses fear that others also may not love them as much as they need to be loved. They are highly functional and seem securely attached until their attachment system is triggered. Then they sense that their spouse is unavailable or views them unfavorably. At the same time they view themselves as unworthy, undesirable, unsure of their own abilities, and uncertain about their value as a person. They fear their spouse doesn't want to be as close as they want.

Gregory missed his wife when she was gone all day, and he felt a mixture of longing for closeness mixed with a tinge of anger. "Where have you been all day? I tried calling your cell phone, but you must have turned it off. You just don't care about me when you are off doing your own thing. I don't want to have dinner with you now." No matter what they do to please others, anxious people like Gregory feel that they are never as winsome or as valued as they would like to be.

When anxious people marry, they experience their spouse's love as unreliable and unpredictable. Sometimes it will feel warm and close, and other times disconnected and distant. The love they want so much is like a slippery bar of soap—one minute they have it and the next they don't. "Do you still love me? Is everything still okay between us?" they frequently ask. Their greatest fear is being abandoned, because they don't believe they can restore a lost love. Sometimes they try to control love, trying hard to make love happen. They fall in love quickly and long to marry quickly so as to "capture" their loved one, then live in a state of anxiety that they will lose their spouse. They can't imagine living without close connectedness. So they make an even greater effort toward closeness and cling to it even harder.

Deep down they doubt their worthiness. One wife once said, "I don't know why my husband stays with me. He is such a patient man. I wouldn't blame him if one day he just gets sick and tired of my neediness and leaves me."

Because of their desperate need for intimacy, anxious people react to any disruption in several ways. One way is to become the *peacemaker*. Make no waves. Don't do anything that will cause your wife to be mad—she might withdraw her love and affection.

Henry describes it this way: "I don't know what to do when I feel she is disappointed in me. My stomach churns inside. I'm so afraid she will leave me. So I quickly apologize—I'm always willing to take the blame. I don't share my true feelings because she might get mad at me. I just can't handle that." Afraid of being rejected, these spouses don't assert themselves, nor are they totally honest about their feelings. Sometimes they fear venturing too far out into the world by themselves, and so they often have difficulty making a decision lest it is a wrong one that leaves them *alone*.

An anxious wife, when discussing a problem with her husband, doubts his willingness or ability to understand or respond sensitively. Anticipating and interpreting her husband's behavior as unresponsive, she may come to feel angry and hostile toward her husband and cling to her hurt long after a fight.

Whenever they sense that their spouse's attentiveness is diverted elsewhere, anxious husbands and wives can often overreact. They accuse, criticize, blame, punish, and are often unable to be soothed by their spouse's returned presence. They say things like, "Where have you been? I've been waiting for you." "You just don't care about me. I'm just not important to you anymore." "You knew this would be hurtful to me, yet you went ahead anyway."

"I scan my relationship," admitted Miranda. "If I sense that my husband is mad at me, then I rush in to get him to like me. I long to be close, but so often fear that he is mad at me. Because if he is mad at me, I feel like I'm in trouble. And that means he doesn't like me. So, when I need my husband close, I make sure he is happy. I rush to take care of him. Then he is happy and content, and I know he is not mad at me. At that point I am safe. But I am not really emotionally connected with him. I am left feeling empty and alone."

Miranda described what it was like to be empty and alone: "I feel very disappointed and sad. I tell myself that I need to be self-sufficient, to take care of myself. So I try to convince myself that I don't need a close connection with my husband. But I never believe it. I long for that closeness."

A long pause. "But it seems impossible to have him be there no matter what. It seems like I won't ever be able to relax and say, 'Aah, he's here, right here beside me.' Instead, I am forever scanning the horizon and working to make him love me."

Another long, thoughtful pause. "Feeling safe without earning and working for his love and affection feels foreign. It feels scary; it's very unsafe to just sit back and trust that he will love me without my doing anything."

Avoidant Attachment Style: Connected Carefully

Like anxious people, avoidants have also not experienced consistent support and closeness from their caregivers. Instead of becoming insecure and clingy, they hold a negative and often cynical view of others. They are uncomfortable with emotional closeness, often saying they don't need it. Because they don't feel confident about relying on others for comfort, they become self-reliant and redirect or suppress their attachment-related thoughts, feelings, and, behaviors.[4]

These people have repeatedly experienced rejection and unavailability in those close to them. Their attachment needs have been denied or avoided. Avoidants distrust others and so limit their dependence on them. As children, they were taught not to cry or display negative or needy feelings.

When hope for emotional responsiveness is lost, attachment needs are suppressed and substituted with tasks, possessions, and accomplishments. Avoidant spouses tend to move away from any expression of emotion that might trigger a sense of longing, hurt, or pain. When they or their partners become agitated, as in a fight, they tend to stay detached and unemotional, redirecting the emotions surrounding closeness and intimacy. In this way they tend neither to seek nor give support when they or their partners need comfort. Their spouses experience them as unemotional, unromantic, cold, and aloof.

Many avoidants are not conscious of their disconnection to closeness and strong emotions. Because tasks and accomplishments keep their attention, they get up each day and get their day's work done. They even value being considered logical, stable, and unemotional. But, if they paused long enough, they would probably admit that they sincerely desire to be more balanced in their emotions and to experience greater closeness with their spouse and others.

When marital problems arise, avoidants doubt that their efforts to get their partner's attention will succeed. So they divert attention away from the conflict and attachment issues. They show no anxiety and are not especially supportive. It is interesting to note that, even though avoidants may show no outward emotional expression, when hooked up to an instrument that measures physiological changes, they are just as physiologically aroused as their partners. After a fight, avoidants do not feel more anger or view their spouse less positively, even though they behave less warmly and supportively during the fight. They don't allow themselves to feel too deeply one way or the other.

Some interesting subgroups here are worth noting:

Strong Leaders

These are independent men and women who are adventurous, independent leaders with a strong presence. They are self-contained, often workaholics, who value their career and independence. Their families often fall into second place in their priorities, after the person's accomplishments, tasks, and activities. Often they will glibly dismiss their spouse's or children's feelings but, when pushed against the wall, they will explode and become angry because they do not have a healthy way of dealing with their own deep emotions.

Gentle Tinkerers

These men faithfully go about their work and are honest and dependable. They are devoted husbands and fathers who look forward to coming home to tinker with the car in the garage or watch the football game on the weekend while barbecuing. They talk best with their wives while doing a task. They listen to their wives' stories with an even-keeled emotional tone. They try to "fix" the problems their wives present and are logical and focused on problem solving, expressing no real highs and no real lows. But they have a protective coating around their hearts. They seem to believe that they don't need to feel deeply or get carried away with emotions. Their self-protection has become familiar and comfortable. They have learned to handle their wives' constant complaining and nagging . . . by letting it roll off like water off a duck's back.

Tough Cookies

Sometimes women who are avoidants can be perceived and labeled as "tough cookies." That means they are seen as women of independent thought and action who don't show much compassion or tolerance of so-called mushy emotions. They have good friends and do well socially. They work hard and accomplish much, yet they are uncomfortable with certain attachment emotions, fearful of getting too close or allowing someone to be dependent on them. They prefer independent and self-sufficient friends and children. They are usually the ones who tell their children, "No need to cry; stand up straight; don't be so clingy."

FEARFUL ATTACHMENT STYLE: CONNECTED CAUTIOUSLY

Fearfuls do desire closeness but are deeply afraid of it. For them, being close also means getting hurt. Closeness has been both the source of comfort and the source of pain. To deal with this ambivalence, cautiously connected people often display contradictory attachment behaviors. They sometimes seem self-sufficient like a carefully connected person, but then switch and become clingy and dependent. Other times they do both at once, reaching for closeness with one hand while pushing away and punishing with the other. This leaves their partner utterly confused.

How does this style arise? As with the others, it is formed primarily through early attachment relationships. The early caregiver to whom they turned was supposed to love and care for them and be their safe haven. But for some reason, the caretaker was unable to fill this role. Perhaps she was preoccupied with her own relationship turmoil (often in second marriages), was an alcoholic, or had some mental illness. Basically, he was inconsistent, depressed, and even abusive—emotionally, physically, or sexually. This creates a paradoxical situation for such a child: Those who love you hurt you the most. Later in life this paradox is transferred to their marriage.

How do fearful spouses fare in marriage? When this style of relating is brought into a marriage, the fearful spouse has great difficulty trusting her mate for comfort and love, and she has an even more difficult time trusting when that spouse does come close. More often than not, the cautiously connected spouse assesses his partner's behaviors as being intentionally hurtful or betraying, and distorts the partner's motives. The cautiously connected spouse will cling, protest, and demand their spouse's attention but then, realizing the potential danger, will stop and pull away, creating a constant state of "push-pull." The longing for being cherished is intertwined with the fear of being hurt and rejected. One wife expressed it this way: "When I kiss my husband, I am drawn to his lips, but I fear that his kiss will bite."

When her husband came close and tried to show some understanding, this wife would pull away and not talk to him for days. "It is terrifying to find him so close to my heart," she would explain.

Listen to Jacob's very similar experience of his marriage.

"Because of other relationships, I bring to this one an untrusting suspiciousness. I somehow believe that my wife will eventually hurt me . . . so I better be alert to the signs and not be taken as a fool." Jacob was obsessed with the idea that Tanya, his wife of two and a half years, would one day abandon him.

"My scanner is always on," Jacob admitted to Tanya. "I scan the airwaves for signs that you will betray me. I fear that I'll do something to push you away and that eventually I'll come to find out that you don't care about me." Jacob likened his experience to a man who had been attacked by a shark. "I scan the water for the fins. I have not had enough experiences to feel *Yes, she won't hurt me or leave me.* When I risk and reach out to her and she does something that hurts me, I tell myself, *See? She will eventually let you down, so don't be a fool to trust her!*"

Hurts in the past set up spouses like Jacob to be hypervigilant in their relationships, and hurts in their present relationship merely serve to confirm that no relationships are safe. It's much safer to be on the lookout for trouble.

Is there healing for such a destructive attachment style? Yes there is! But fear can prevent such people from experiencing the healing touch they desperately need. It's like trying to convince someone that a venomous snake can actually be of great comfort to her, say as a pet, if only she would hold it close. We shudder at the thought! The idea that a snake could ever be the source of comfort is inconceivable. In this sense, those with severe cautiously connected feelings would shudder at the thought of truly trusting someone with their heart. If this describes you, then read on—there is hope, even for the worst of our fears.

It Makes Sense

Examining your relationship through the lens of attachment can be tremendously helpful in building a safe haven marriage. It helps you understand and manage how each of you interacts, feels, and behaves in your marriage. This "depathologizes" each of you. In other words, neither of you is the needy, undifferentiated, sick, or immature partner. There is nothing wrong with you if you react with caution when in close relationship with your spouse. Past experiences have shaped the way you attach and make you feel vulnerable in your present circumstances. Thankfully, with understanding you can move beyond this.

This is what happened to Todd and Angela after they had read a draft version of this chapter. Angela turned to me (Sharon) and said, "Now I get it. I've brought a fear from my past into our marriage that Todd will not love me as much as I want him to and that he will be disappointed when he really gets to know me. So each time he expresses disappointment, I have a big reaction. I get so angry and defensive. How and why I've been reacting now make perfect sense to both of us."

"Yes," added Todd, "she's definitely anxious in her attachment style. And since I'm more avoidant, the combination hasn't exactly helped our relationship. When she tries to come close to me by clinging and wanting these intense talk sessions, I pull away. I feel overwhelmed and suffocated. And because I don't always know what I'm feeling, I only become more frustrated and angry. And I avoid her more. I'm beginning to feel a bit more hopeful that we can overcome this difference!"

CORRECTIVE EXPERIENCES

Here's the good news: You don't have to be stuck in a particular attachment style for the rest of your life. As you reach out and risk new experiences, you can learn how to trust others and find support, comfort, and protection. Those who become firmly set in their beliefs about themselves and others and are unwilling to change will have a harder time incorporating new information and experiences. They will more likely stay anxious, fearful, or avoidant in their attachments.

Couples can learn how to interact with each other and find points of contact to overcome their basic differences. They can find ways of working around their attachment styles, thus reshaping them as they encounter new experiences. With the right frame of mind, these experiences can become emotionally corrective. In other words, as we grow and mature, we are able to move toward a more secure way of being. As we do so, we begin to view ourselves as lovable, to see others as safe with good intentions, and to find out that consistent closeness is a viable possibility.

We would like to share with you an example of such a transformation from the research we are doing. One couple in particular stands out. The wife has an attachment style that is fearful while the husband is avoidant. As a fearful, the wife tends to long for closeness but fears being hurt, so she draws close to him and then pushes away just like a swimmer would do when making a turn against the poolside wall. She married a man who tends to stay at arm's length. This makes him emotionally unavailable, proving that people are not always "there for you when you need them." And when she emotionally pushes him away, it proves to him that love is unpredictable and suffocating.

It would seem that this combination of attachment styles would not make for an emotionally close marriage. But quite to the contrary! They scored quite high on the Haven of Safety Scale. Despite their different styles, they still perceived their marriage to be a safe haven, and in fact they felt quite securely attached.

How was this possible, given their opposing attachment styles?

Amazed by what we discovered, we went back and read their personal comments regarding their relationship. The wife wrote, "My husband is devoted to me and our marriage. He has stood with me through life's challenges and difficulties and has always been so faithful and helpful. It took several years of him sticking with me before I was really able to know he meant it. *I have come to trust that he is there for me.*"

Now listen to what her husband wrote: "My wife has become my best friend and the only one with whom I can share all of my thoughts and dreams. *I trust her with my heart.*"

Read the last sentences in italics. This couple has obviously had a powerful healing experience. As a basically fearful person, the wife has lived with both the yearning and the terror of intimacy, and while the husband is avoidant, he was nevertheless consistently trustworthy and never abandoned her. She had learned, through experience, that he can be trusted no matter what. His independence never meant that he didn't care. And despite the history of fears they had each brought into their marriage, they were able to find a safe haven with each other. It may have taken them many years of sticking with each other to reach this point, but making a commitment to give their relationship priority over everything else won the day for them.

This may sound like a fairy tale, but it is real. We respect their courage to search each other out despite the dragons they both had to face to finally reach one another. We pray that this will give you hope as you read on.

REFLECTION QUESTIONS

1. Following is a simple test to assess your attachment style.[5] As you review the above attachment styles (you may have to reread them several times to really grasp their differences), you might be concerned because you don't clearly fit into any one of these styles all the time. You can be specifically one attachment style, or have a bit of two styles. Most of you will discover that under some conditions you are, for example, certainly connected, but when hurt, your vulnerabilities are touched and you become uncertain, cautious, or careful in how you react to your spouse.

How do you rate on a secure attachment style scale? Circle the response that best represents you:

It is easy for me to become emotionally close to others. I am comfortable depending on others and having others depend on me. I don't worry about being alone or having others not accept me.

Not like me at all		Somewhat like me			Very much like me	
1	2	3	4	5	6	7

How do you rate on an anxious attachment style scale? Circle the number that represents you:

I want to be emotionally intimate with others, but I often find that others are reluctant to get as close as I would like. I am uncomfortable being without close relationships, and I sometimes worry that others don't value me as much as I value them.

Not like me at all		Somewhat like me			Very much like me	
1	2	3	4	5	6	7

How do you rate on an avoidant attachment style scale? Circle the number that represents you:

> *I am somewhat uncomfortable being close to others. I am comfortable without close relationships. It is very important to me to feel independent and self-sufficient, and I prefer not to depend on others or have others depend on me.*

Not like me at all		Somewhat like me			Very much like me	
1	2	3	4	5	6	7

How do you rate on a fearful attachment style scale? Circle the number that best represents you:

> *I am uncomfortable getting close to others. I want emotionally close relationships, but I find it difficult to trust others completely or to depend on them. I worry that I will be hurt if I allow myself to become too close to others.*

Not like me at all		Somewhat like me			Very much like me	
1	2	3	4	5	6	7

2. What would you say most accurately describes your attachment style? How do you respond when you perceive your spouse to be emotionally unavailable or unresponsive, or when your spouse doesn't understand your point of view?

3. What is your spouse's attachment style? How does your spouse respond when hurt?

4. What attachment style fits your parents or significant people in your life? How have these experiences affected your understanding of yourself and the safety of intimacy?

5. How can you grow to foster a more secure way of being in your marriage?

Part Two

SAFE HAVEN INTERRUPTIONS

Chapter 6

PATTERNS THAT LEAVE COUPLES EMOTIONALLY DISCONNECTED

The part of me that most longs for connection is left painfully alone. When I reach for you, you slip away, so I reach for you again. But my reaching seems only to make you more unattainable.

—ANONYMOUS CLIENT

*R*emember our prince and princess from the last chapter? Suppose that when the couple first laid eyes on each other, the princess thought he was her prince, and he thought she was definitely his princess. Then, before long, neither was quite so sure. Both wondered whether the other was a dragon to be fought or a loved one to be treasured. This is the reality that faces all of us as we try to connect with another person in the intimacy of marriage.

Let's return to the castle scene. Yelling from the tower window, the princess declares, "You'd better not be the dragon, or I'll have to attack you!"

Jumping off his horse, the prince finds shelter behind a tree just beyond the castle moat. He cautiously peers out and shouts, "If you strike me, I shall have to defend myself."

"Go ahead, buddy boy," the princess responds. "Defend all you want, but I will not let you hurt me—not even a little. I will keep attacking."

"I cannot allow myself to be continually attacked. If you can't see who I really am, then I will need to withdraw from here to a safe place," the prince explains.

"Fine," the princess declares, "but then I will follow you in hot pursuit. I won't let you leave me here alone!" Her voice softens, "I can't let you hide because you've awakened something in me."

Becoming bolder, the prince moves briefly into the open. Puzzled, he asks, "If you don't want me to leave but want me to come closer to you, then why do you have to attack me?" Then he quickly ducks behind the tree again, not knowing what her response will be.

The princess answers, "If you've really come to claim my love, then why do you withdraw and hide at the slightest threat? I wouldn't need to pursue you if I could really see you for who you are."

The prince ponders this for a moment, then responds, "But if I stand out in the open, I might get hurt." And then under his breath he mutters, "Even great knights don't like getting hurt—especially not by princesses!"

MARITAL PATTERNS AND CYCLES: THE DANCE

This fairy tale illustrates the way couples often interact when dealing with a misunderstanding: They fight to be seen, understood, and valued. To change the metaphor for a moment, the way couples exchange differences of opinion or argue is a form of dance. They dance around in an attempt to be acknowledged. Counselors call this an interactional pattern. It is the dance inside the emotional fight.

Imagine a husband and a wife on a dance floor. His arm is around her waist; her hand is resting on his shoulder. As one spouse steps back, the other steps forward. When one spouse steps in one direction, the other responds and moves accordingly. Gliding across the dance floor they are sometimes in rhythm, and other times they may get caught in a hurtful tangle.

Whether couples act more like princes and princesses or ballroom dancers, the point is that husbands and wives are intricately connected in a pattern of interaction that becomes habitual over the course of a marriage—it is deeply entrenched. Once it gets ahold of them, it is likely to stay in place.

THE REAL PROBLEM IS NOT THE FIGHTING, BUT THE EMOTIONAL DISCONNECTION

In fact, the *way* couples cope with their differences and conflicts—this inter-actional dance—is more important than the specific issues they fight about. As you will recall, the main theme of this book is that couples need to learn how to stay emotionally connected if their marriages are to be safe havens. It is the pattern of fighting they get stuck in while arguing that disintegrates the shelter of their home.

Some cycles become rigid and hinder the fostering of a secure bond. The reason is obvious: These cycles have the power to keep couples emotionally disconnected. Once locked in a rigid cycle, husbands and wives are not able to access each other emotionally. They become limited in their ability to respond sensitively to one another.

Once couples get stuck in this same rigid cycle (and it can last a lifetime), neither is able to pull back and talk about what is happening. They cannot find an exit. The cycle moves them farther and farther away from each other. One spouse will blame their partner's upbringing, character, inability to have emotions (usually directed at the male), or inability to control their emotions (usually directed at the female). The cycle they are both stuck in is damaging to the relationship bond and tends to take on a life of its own.

Each partner contributes to the cycle, or dance—because, as the saying goes, "It takes two to tango." And each is affected by the negative behavior. In this sense, both husband and wife must accept responsibility for the recurring pattern that keeps them emotionally separated. Let's try to discern the unique pattern of interaction that keeps husbands and wives from connecting.

WHAT TRIGGERS ARGUMENTS?

What turns an innocent conversation, a quiet stroll, a guileless comment, or a team effort in the kitchen into an argument? It seems that a conversation is always one sentence and one emotion away from turning into an argument. It is often the case that arguments start when one spouse is hurt because he feels unseen, misunderstood, and devalued.

When you perceive your partner to be emotionally unavailable, unresponsive, or not worthwhile, your attachment system clicks in. You protest the
comment or act in an attempt to get your spouse to be more caring and attentive. A combination of the manner in which you do it, and what your
response in turn means to and triggers in your spouse, starts an argument. In
an attempt for you to get your spouse (and your spouse to get you) to be more
caring and attentive, an argument begins.

There are four events that make a spouse feel their partner was not there
for them and can trigger an argument: *criticism, unfair requests, cumulative
aggravations,* and *rejection.*[1]

First is *criticism.* Critical remarks feel like put-downs. They devalue us.

Second is a *demand* (or request) that is perceived as unfair and unreasonable. Your spouse asks you to do something that you don't want to do because
you feel it doesn't make sense. For example, Miguel calls up his wife, Kelly,
late one afternoon and asks her to go to the accountant's office before it closes
to pick up the paychecks for their employees. The problem is that Kelly is on
her way to pick up her sister from the airport.

"Miguel, you're putting me in a tough spot. You procrastinated all day, and
now you want me to pick up the ball that you have dropped," Kelly says.
"You're being unreasonable!"

But Miguel doesn't see it that way. He responds, "You are never there when
I need you. I am always carrying the full load of this household and our business, and I get no help whatsoever!"

Kelly thinks Miguel is making an unreasonable demand. Miguel thinks
Kelly is being inconsiderate by not doing what he asks. Impasse! Thus begins
an argument that may last for days.

Third, conflicts are also triggered by what are called *cumulative aggravations.* These are annoying, frustrating things that one's spouse does repeatedly
and over time. They get interpreted as inconsiderate, thoughtless, and unkind
gestures. For example, Bud keeps forgetting to transfer his wash into the
dryer. When Lindsay goes to the washer, she invariably finds a moldy, smelly
bundle. This aggravates her to no end. Another example: Kareem considers
Shannon's repeated lateness as a manifestation of her lack of respect for him.
She's always late, even though he has carefully communicated how he feels. It

becomes an accumulated aggravation. Also, Brandon's lack of creativity on Valentine's Day, birthdays, and anniversaries takes on a negative meaning for his wife, May, who interprets his boring, predictable gifts as a lack of love.

A fourth trigger is *rejection*. A partner's failure to respond in a caring and considerate manner can feel like rejection. Take Roland and Dorothy, for example. Roland is sitting in the Jacuzzi one evening. Dorothy finally finishes the dishes and goes to join Roland. As soon as she settles down into the steaming water, Roland reaches over to kiss and caress her. Dorothy physically pushes him away.

"Just give me a minute to unwind. You've been sitting here for ten minutes, but I've been working. I need a little time to relax."

Roland interprets this as rejection and feels hurt. "No matter what I do, you push me away. I'm tired of trying to get close to you!"

So much for a loving evening. Yet a little consideration from both partners could have made their time in the Jacuzzi an affectionate and tender experience for both of them!

THE EMOTIONS THAT ARE TRIGGERED

Tess has spent the weekend helping her mother clean out the house after her father was moved into a convalescent home. Now she sits at the dining room table, exhausted. Her husband, Esteban, dishes up the food.

"This is so wonderful. Thank you, Esteban," Tess says appreciatively. "Well, what did everyone do while I was at Grandma's house?"

"Dad had friends over," pipes the youngest, innocently enough.

"Oh, really?" Tess takes another bite to hide her surprise, then looks at Esteban. "Who?"

"Oh, just the guys from the delivery department at the office," Esteban reluctantly confesses.

"What!" Tess is instantly offended. "You know I don't like you hanging out with those guys!"

"It's not such a big deal, Tess. Don't get bent out of shape. Anyway, what am I supposed to do while you are gone—stay home alone?"

"What do you mean, *stay home alone?*" Tess stands up from the table, her face red and her lips tight. "You are so immature!" she hisses at her husband. "It's obvious that you're sorry you're married, because now you can't do what you want when you want to!"

Can you identify with Esteban and Tess? Can you think of a time when a conversation escalated quickly into an argument? Suddenly you felt hurt, mad. Maybe what your spouse said was a criticism, an unfair demand, or a rejection. The words that were spoken felt like an intentionally hurtful attack. How could anybody be so insensitive?

Emotions well up inside your stomach and boil to the surface. Your feelings of disappointment, frustration, hurt, and anger become all-consuming. The only thoughts that run through your mind are, *How could she have done that?* or, *He is just so insensitive and selfish!* or, *She never considers me and what's best for us!*

You say things that take even you by surprise. And what are you trying to accomplish with your reactive words and actions? Your anger hopes to serve three purposes:

1. You want *to communicate* how hurt you are. In a way you are rebuking him for saying or doing what he did.

2. You want *to get a response* from your spouse. You want to show her how wrong she has been and how she should change.

3. You want *to motivate* him to be more thoughtful, caring, sensitive, emotionally available, and responsive.

HOW CAN YOU RESPOND?

"Maybe I'm making things worse," you tell yourself, "but honestly, what am I supposed to do?" Somehow your wife's behavior or reaction signals that she isn't there for you. Or you can't help feeling as if your husband doesn't understand or care about you. How can you respond?

There seem to be only a few options available. And you may find it interesting that these options are actually physiologically connected to your central nervous system. We all react in our emotional lives in much the same way we react to danger in our everyday lives. Our options are to fight, flee, freeze, or tend and care.

Of course you can up the ante and *fight* with a loud, assertive, and convincing argument. You can fight to get your spouse's attention and get him to understand your perspective. You can fight to show that you are not unlovable. You can fight to get your spouse to see how he has hurt you, or to get her to recognize her wrong behavior and change.

You can also *flee* and avoid further confrontation. If defending yourself hasn't worked, you can simply get out of the fight's path and withdraw. In this way, you are able to protect your heart.

You can *freeze* and stop in your tracks. Maybe you see a fight forming on the horizon like a tropical storm, and you determine that the best way to avoid it is to batten down the hatches emotionally and refuse to move. If you are not noticed, possibly the fight will pass you by or dwindle away. This way you protect your heart and avoid a battle.

Or you can do a *combination* of all three. You can attempt to come close, but then freeze and pull back to protect yourself.

Studies are beginning to show us that there is a fourth way of responding, called *tend and care.* Here the spouse, usually the wife, clicks into a nurturing mode. She cooks, cleans, grooms, and tends to the needs of others as a way of warding off the argument, bringing peace and connection, and soothing herself.

Of course there is yet one more option. It may sound more difficult than it really is, but it is the healthiest. In a safe haven marriage, you can approach your spouse with *secure* confidence and assurance that when you begin to talk about the issue at hand, both of you will be heard, understood, and valued. Here you are able to identify your needs and longings and appropriately share them and ask for them to be met.

FOUR HORSEMEN THAT FUEL THE CYCLE

Before we move on to specific responses, it is essential that we consider four key behaviors that are highly detrimental to emotional connectedness and the fostering of a safe haven marriage. John Gottman calls these four interactions between wives and husbands the "Four Horsemen of the Apocalypse" (see Revelation 6:2–8). These four attitudes—*criticism, contempt, defensiveness,* and *stonewalling*—will destroy a marriage as sure as the four horsemen will ultimately destroy the earth. These attitudes must be avoided if you are to prevent a destructive cycle from becoming entrenched in your marriage, and they must be changed if you are ever to break such a cycle.

Criticism—The White Horse

No marriage can survive a constant barrage of criticism. And before we consider what this really means, we have to avoid confusion between "complaints" and "criticisms." One can register a complaint without being critical. And we're talking about criticism here, not just moaning about what your partner does or says, or expressing your disagreement with your partner's opinion. Criticism goes a step further and *personally attacks the character of your partner.*

A complaint says, "I don't like it when you leave your smelly socks on the couch. Can you please put them in the dirty clothes basket?" Actually, expressing one's frustration and anger in a direct, productive way can be healthy for a marriage, if the complaint is legitimate. (Adding an occasional "please" also helps.)

Criticism, in contrast, says, "You are a slob just like your father, always leaving your smelly socks on the couch! I'm sick to death of you!" Here you express your complaint, but you do so in attack mode. Don't be surprised if your husband doesn't change his behavior. Your critical words are useless and only serve to heighten the conflict.

Feelings, frustrations, and needs should be shared in a straightforward manner that doesn't attack the character of the other person. Unfortunately, even this may not succeed unless it is communicated in the context of a safe haven with an attitude that says, "I am here to love you no matter what." If you express your concerns and your spouse still ignores what you're saying, you may need to work a little harder at developing the love connection.

It doesn't take much to turn a complaint into a criticism. All you have to do is add some version of: "What's your problem, anyway?" Criticisms are broad, generalized statements such as, "You *never* help me with anything! You always seem to find plenty of time to do your own stuff, but I can't remember the last time you had time to help me."

Criticisms often contain a tinge of being let down or of having trust betrayed: "I don't ask much of you. I trusted you to pick up the dry cleaning, but you didn't. I really needed you to do this one tiny thing for me, and you just blew me off. How could you do this to me? You just never make me a priority. I can't believe how inconsiderate you are!"

Somehow you need to break the cycle of criticism without surrendering your right to be truthful about your feelings. And sometimes the subtle difference between complaining and criticizing can be difficult to grasp. What can be helpful is to remind yourself that no one else is to blame for the way you feel. You are responsible for how you express your discontent.

The key to reasonable communication is to own your emotions, to share what you feel without blaming others. Then state what you would like to see happen in as clear a way as possible. The reaction cited in the example of forgotten dry cleaning could be restated in a healthier way as follows: "While I sometimes feel that I am not high on your priorities, I realize that you are also a busy person." (Always give the benefit of the doubt—you will also benefit.) "So could you please pick up the dry cleaning on your way home from work tomorrow? If you like, I can call you before you leave and remind you." (Offering a constructive solution is a way of saying, "I am reaching out to find a way to move beyond this impasse.")

Contempt—The Fiery Red Horse

Contempt takes criticism one step beyond by not only attacking the character of your spouse, but also aiming an arrow right at the heart of your partner's sense of self-respect.

How does contempt take root? Failed attempts to gain the understanding and responsiveness of your spouse may have caused you to mull over negative and demeaning thoughts and feelings about her: "You are *so* stupid, *so* incompetent, *so* useless, *such* a fool!" Thoughts such as these magnify your spouse's negatives and mask all your partner's good qualities. The loss of admiration and respect for one's spouse is the reason that contempt is so dangerous to the marital interactional cycle.

Once again we are indebted to John Gottman for some insights here. He states that there are four ways to recognize when you are expressing contempt toward your spouse:

1. Insults and Name-Calling. I am sure you can list the names you call your spouse when you are fighting. The names might look harmless if I wrote them down here, but they are able to do great damage. Refuse to say such things as *stupid, idiot, lazy, selfish, just like your father/mother,* and any similar put-downs.

2. Hostile Humor. We've all heard this kind of thinly disguised cruelty. It is sometimes sarcastic, sometimes ironic, and sometimes a hurtful jab. Maybe a husband makes a joke about his wife when she's on the verge of tears and trivializes her pain. Maybe a wife refuses to have a serious conversation with her husband, always looking for a snappy comeback. Some couples' conversations are riddled with criticism and contempt couched as comic relief. It isn't funny.

3. Mockery. This is where you make fun of, ridicule, or put down your spouse. For example, one spouse might say, "Honey, I really want to help you get through this big project." The other responds mockingly, "Oh, yeah, sure. After making scrapbooks with the kids all day? I'm sure you'll be a huge help putting together an executive PowerPoint presentation."

4. Body Language. After watching hours of videos of couples, one researcher found several common body expressions that communicate contempt. See if you recognize any of these: sneering, rolling the eyes, curling up the lip, or deep sighing. Wives and husbands are quick to pick up any incongruence between what is said and body language. Often it is the inconsistency that communicates contempt.

For example, a husband says to his wife, "Darling, I'm sorry. Please tell me how you feel." But as his wife begins to speak, he steals a quick look at his watch, glances in the mirror, and straightens his tie, poised to rush out the door. She hears him saying, "I don't care about what you have to say. I've got better things to do than listen to you whine. I ignore you because you are overly emotional, don't make sense, and are pretty much wasting my time right at the moment."

Defensiveness—The Black Horse

This dangerous horse follows closely behind contempt. Our natural response to being attacked is to protect ourselves and go on the defensive. When we feel threatened, we also feel justified in raising a shield or wearing protective armor. To defend ourselves when attacked is an instinctive response.

Let's return momentarily to our fairy tale. The prince feels perfectly warranted to take up a safe position behind a tree near the castle. What else can he do? Even brave knights don't like being hurt. But as the prince takes a defensive, protective stance, the conflict is escalated rather than resolved or defused. And no matter how justified he feels about his defensive position, the princess is only going to feel more afraid. A self-protective stance can never be a "connection" stance. It drives couples apart; it doesn't draw them together.

What does defensiveness sound like? "That is *not* what I meant." "You have it *all wrong.*" "I know it looks this way *on the outside,* but I was just about to . . ."

The body language of a defensive person can be a false and misleading smile. The edges of the mouth may curl up, but the eyes betray the feelings—they don't light up. The defended body shifts from side to side, as though avoiding a punch. Arms are folded across the chest, forming a breastplate; hands fiddle around the neck or rub the eyes to clear the vision. And the defensive one nearly always looks away when he talks.

Defensiveness in ourselves isn't all that difficult to detect—our spouses are usually happy to point it out. When that happens, let's try not to become defensive about our defensiveness!

Stonewalling—The Pale Horse

Stonewalling simply means that one spouse stops responding to the other, putting up an impenetrable, invisible wall. When people stonewall, they no longer resort to criticizing or demonstrating contempt, and they move beyond the need to defend themselves. They pull back, turn inward, and shut down, leaving their wife or husband out in the cold, in a relationship without a safe haven.

The pale horseman adds poison to the emotional cycle. Stonewalling can have a deadly effect on a marriage relationship. It speaks powerfully to the other spouse. What messages does it send? *You really don't count. You don't matter to me. You're not even worth fighting with.* Disengaging from any meaningful interaction causes us to become aloof, distant, detached, and seemingly uncaring. In effect, we have become indifferent to the relationship.

We've avoided categorizing certain behaviors as typically male or female, but the fact is that most stonewallers are men. According to John Gottman, this is true because men become overwhelmed by the physiology of something called "emotional flooding"—they just don't know how to identify and deal with their feelings and often fear losing control. Emotional negativity, whether in the form of criticism, contempt, or defensiveness, becomes overwhelming to them.

Men typically don't know how to face hot emotions head-on without exploding with anger, so they learn to avoid the attacks. We males control our physiology by withdrawing and moving away to a safe place, out of the reach of conflict. The prince, therefore, could easily abandon the shelter of a tree and hole up in a cave somewhere.

Wives usually respond by keeping up the attack, criticizing their husbands or yelling at them, and explaining again and again how it feels when their husbands shut down. These wives miss what their husbands are really trying to tell them when they stonewall. "I can't handle your hostility. I'm afraid I'll lose control and do something in response to your criticism and contemptuous attitude that I'll later regret."

Meanwhile, stonewalling husbands are unable to hear their wives say, "You have no idea how scared I feel when you go and hide in your cave. It tells me that you really don't care about me or how I feel." The cycle becomes increasingly destructive with each episode of stonewalling. In fact, a cycle where the wife pursues with contempt and the husband stonewalls in response is a predictor of divorce, according to John Gottman.

THE INTERACTIONAL DANCE

Let's return to Esteban and Tess and try to understand their cycle. Tess has several options available as she considers how to respond to Esteban. After hearing that Esteban spent time with the buddies whom she clearly disapproves of, she gets angry and approaches Esteban with emotional intensity. She chooses to *fight*. She pursues him for an explanation. She wants him to see how wrong he was. The only way she thinks she can make him understand how upset she feels is to attack and criticize him.

In return Esteban takes the next step in their dance. He doesn't move close and say to Tess, "I know you're upset that I hung out with guys you don't like, and I want to share my thoughts about it with you. But to do that, I need you to not criticize or demean me." No, Esteban feels she is being unfair, judging him and his buddies. He feels overwhelmed by her attack and so he takes a step back and defends himself.

The next step is Tess's. Tess does not take a step back, pause, and try to understand Esteban. Instead, she feels him pulling away from her and so she increases the heat and becomes more critical and angry. She takes one big step forward. Esteban, in return, defends himself, stepping back farther and eventually shutting down and withdrawing. This is the basic pursue-withdraw cycle that is at the core of many arguments.

THE PURSUER

The pursuer and the withdrawer are like a porcupine and a tortoise. The porcupine has sharp quills it raises and displays when it is threatened. The tortoise has a thick, hard shell and is more than happy to disappear inside it, where no porcupine quills can reach his sensitive areas. Let's take a closer look. Christie had once found Ruben's more quiet demeanor comforting and anchoring. But now it frustrates her.

Christie begins, "I want Ruben to be more self-disclosing about what's going on in his life. It hurts me when I ask him a question and he gives me a one- or two-word answer. So I probe him and ask him more questions. It's like I am reaching for him, but I can't touch him."

"What is that like, Christie, not to be able to reach Ruben?" I (Sharon) asked.

"I feel frustrated, really mad. It really hurts."

"And what happens when you feel mad and frustrated?"

"I probe him. I have to follow him around the house to get him to listen to me. And it makes me mad, because I have to work so hard to get him to talk to me. But I go after him anyway—he doesn't have the right to shut me out the way he does."

When spouses sense that their mates are withdrawn, they pursue, often using anger and criticism in an attempt to get their spouse to emotionally engage. A pursuer feels angry and frustrated. Pursuers perceive that the only way to obtain their spouse's attentiveness is to attack, to escalate the emotions. These husbands and wives don't intend to criticize, demean, or be contemptuous. Instead, they long for closeness, to be heard, understood, and valued. But they feel that pursuit is the only means they have for getting the attention of their spouse.

Christie describes it this way: "I feel like I'm out on the street and he's a businessman inside a building. The only way to get seen or be noticed is if I get out my picket sign and pace up and down in front of the office shouting and yelling. Only then, when he looks out of his office window and sees this noisy protester, will he grasp what's going on. Otherwise, he'll ignore me. Walk right past me. Go on with his day and not even notice me."

Most damaging of all may be the way the pursuer presents her case. Often the conversation is initiated in an angry voice. The words are immediate, hot, loud, intense, and sharp. The statements are accusations or criticisms. This is what John Gottman calls "harsh start-ups." These, too, are highly correlated with couples whose marriages end in divorce.

Harsh start-ups in conversation convey immediate anger, disgust, and dislike for the other person. They do not foster safety in the relationship. Instead, they put the pursuer's partner on the immediate defensive. The couple doesn't feel like a team, facing the world together. Instead, the pursued spouse feels like an outsider who has to protect himself from an attack. Sort of like a tortoise assaulted by a porcupine.

A pursuer may ask, "Then what am I supposed to do? Let my spouse get away with what he was doing? Not feel the way I feel?" No, the answer is not to numb one's emotions and become avoidant. That doesn't bring health, nor does it foster a safe haven. It just turns the relationship into a land mine. Once we've buried our hurt and anger, they are likely to explode later, often when we least expect it.

Instead, pursuers need to learn how to recognize emotions and to express them in a more reasonable manner. This is called using our emotional intelligence, and it is of great importance to our relationships.

THE WITHDRAWER

When we're under attack, many of us defend ourselves because we are hurt by our spouse's criticism. We probably feel that our spouse is unjustified in saying what she said, or in criticizing us the way he did. We defend and try to say, "No, that isn't true about me, and furthermore, it hurts that you would think about me that way."

Before long, realizing that there is no point in continuing our defense because the other person is not going to understand us, we withdraw. To reduce the hot emotions and disengage ourselves from the argument, we pull away while shutting down on the inside. We lower the shutters of our heart. We're there physically, maybe even talking in a polite, calm tone of voice. Possibly yelling back and forth. But inside we have shut down, pulled back, and protected ourselves from the porcupine quills.

We are, in essence, saying, "I will never let you hurt me again. I won't let you in, so you can't hurt me."

If your wife starts to talk about something very painful and expresses emotion, you find you have taken a step back and detached yourself from her experience. You might roll your eyes, chalk it up to "emotional irrationality," or slowly tune her out.

Let's listen in on Ruben's experience as a withdrawer. Make note of how he responds when he feels Christie is pursuing him with criticism and anger.

"I try my best to answer her questions, but my answers are never good enough for her. She gets mad at everything I say. We talk, but I don't feel like she hears or understands me. I think to myself, *Have I done wrong? Is she right—am I really a bad person?*"

He continues, "I have to fight certain images she has about me. She says I'm aloof, passive, and unsociable. I have to defend myself. I don't feel safe when she attacks me. So I back away. It's like I can feel myself going into another room. I don't ever let her into that room."

But all withdrawers don't behave the same way. Sometimes a withdrawer will first attack, emotionally exploding before shutting down. He will get in a few angry sentences before pulling back and withdrawing. Others emotionally freeze, refusing to respond.

You Explode Then Withdraw

"Don't let the kids stand so close to the barbecue, David!" Ashley yelled at her husband as he was cooking burgers on the grill.

David wheeled around and glared at his wife. "You are the most negative person I know! Can't we ever get through a weekend without your getting so emotional and bossy?" David exploded. He continued his tirade for about three minutes, telling Ashley how terrible she was. Then he shut down.

Ashley could see the change on her husband's face. His eyes widened, he squeezed his lips tightly together, and he shook his head. Inside, the shutters slammed down, and the lock on his heart clicked shut. He fell silent, turned the burgers, and continued playing with the kids, totally ignoring Ashley. For the rest of that day, for the night and day that followed, David kept to himself, working on his own projects. David has his own style of withdrawing: He attacks, and then he shuts down, pulls away, and sulks.

You Freeze

Paul was never allowed to feel as a child. All feelings were "disciplined out of him," he likes to say. So he has learned to detach his feelings from his daily life. Like everyone else, he dreamed of marriage that would be a safe haven, from which he could pursue a comfortable life. He eventually married Sarah, who was friendly and energetic. She added joy and fun and color to his world. Until, that is, they faced disagreements.

When Sarah showed that she felt hurt, or tried to get her point of view across to Paul, he would freeze. He would stand still in his tracks, not feeling or thinking anything. Somehow he seemed to think that if he stood perfectly still he would be invisible, and that as time passed by, all the troubles and hassles would just pass by or dissolve.

"A little voice inside me," Paul explains, "says that if I react or respond, she will be disappointed in me and leave. So I get very quiet. I guess I'm thinking that maybe she'll calm down and cool off, and it'll all blow over. But it makes her even more angry."

PURSUE-WITHDRAW CYCLES

Different couples engage in pursue-withdraw cycles in several ways. Let's take a look at a few examples.

One Pursues; the Other Withdraws

Daniel and Debra struggled with the pursue-withdraw cycle in yet another way. As Daniel leaned forward in his chair, his brow furrowed, he rubbed his face as if to wipe away the pain. "I wish Debra would trust me," he began. "I'm trying to finish this project at the office so I can get a promotion, and once that's done, I won't have to put in all this overtime. I wish she would just believe that I value her more than my job. Just because I have to put in overtime doesn't mean that she's not my first priority."

Debra sat up straight, keeping her eyes on Daniel, and said, "I don't feel heard! He just doesn't understand how hard it is for me to be alone so much of the time. So I have to fight back. I tell him that he doesn't care and that his work is more important than I am. And you know what? It is! Nothing he does shows me otherwise. I can't change the way I feel. And I feel I am not a priority."

From Debra's point of view, Daniel's absences had come to mean that he didn't care for her. And when she felt alone and uncared for, she panicked and fought back to get him to be emotionally available and responsive.

Daniel sighed and responded, "This is so draining. It makes me want to defend myself. I have to make things clear. I have to say, 'Look! You are still my priority, even though I have to work a lot.' When Debra isn't happy with me, I tell myself, *She's going to escalate this like she always does.* I can sense the escalation coming. I can see her starting to attack me. She comes to prove her point: 'You value your work more than me.' So I have to explain myself, defend myself. I feel trapped. So I just shut her out. And sometimes that means I stay at work, because when I'm at work, I don't have to listen to her!"

Daniel's natural response to Debra's criticism and pursuit was to defend himself. Then, when that failed, he became overwhelmed and so he stonewalled. Daniel's inability to be emotionally accessible caused Debra to pursue more aggressively, hoping to get Daniel to emotionally connect. But Debra is too busy pursuing and criticizing Daniel to be emotionally accessible and responsive herself.

Both Partners Withdraw

Sometimes both partners withdraw. This usually happens because one spouse was the withdrawer, and the pursuer has now given up the fight. Some partners have pursued their spouses for months, if not years, attempting to get the other's emotional attention. Slowly but surely they've lost hope and resigned themselves to the fact that their spouse simply will not respond to their cries. Maybe this is your experience. You have lost hope of things ever changing, and you've slowly pulled back from your pursuit.

You have moved from protest to sadness, then to despair, and now to a detached or resigned stance. You have placed a protective armor around your heart. You now only go through the motions of caring for your spouse, but you no longer demand or expect intimacy. You have come to the conclusion that you and your spouse may never have an emotional connection. This is a sad resignation, a loss of hope, a deep need that has remained unmet. It is indifference—the bitter residue of a broken dream.

Cindy pursued her husband for years and eventually gave up and became a withdrawer. "I can't tell you how long I tried to get him to sit and listen to how I felt about things. He would just say that I was emotional and illogical, and we would get into bigger fights. Finally, I realized I was destroying our relationship by demanding more. We've been married for eighteen years, and he has·not changed, and he is not going to. It's no use trying to get him to understand me. We just end up fighting. I could spend my time hating him and being angry and disappointed. So instead, I guess I have shut down on the inside. I've quit trying."

Both Partners Pursue

On the other hand, some couples never give up. Instead, they develop a volatile style of dealing with conflict. Both speak their minds, both are argumentative, and both spend time trying to convince the other of their side of the debate. They sound like lawyers arguing their case. There is an endless power struggle, and each partner is determined to win. The words shared between them may become cruel, and the wounds can be very deep. This destructive cycle doesn't allow for a time-out where nurturing and understanding can take place. As one wife told me, "If I don't win this argument, then I won't have an edge in the next argument. If he wins all the time, then I will be nothing. I won't have anything to stand on."

Do you recognize any of the pursue-withdraw cycles? Which cycle looks most like yours? How quick do you find yourselves in one of these unpleasant interactions? How difficult is it to exit? Do you turn to your husband at breakfast, ask him to pass the butter, and before you know it you feel criticized? Suddenly you're defending yourself, and he is criticizing you in return. Before long, neither of you talks to the other for the rest of the day. If the reaction is quick and intense, then you are probably in a spin cycle, like a washing machine. All you do is go round and round without any resolve or meaningful reconnection.

ESCALATION CREATES NEW PROBLEMS

When fights escalate and a rigid cycle of pursue-withdraw is in place, the original issue that needed to be dealt with and resolved often gets lost in the spin cycle.

The Initial Problem Gets Lost

Escalation of a conflict creates a new and more intense problem: You begin to argue about who said what. You argue about the argument. You try to clarify what each of you meant and who said what when, but the fight now focuses on how your spouse misunderstands and misreads your statements. Everything is taken out of context, and the argument heads off on a rabbit trail about how you parent, do business, treat the in-laws, take care of the budget, or keep the house. None of these issues are what you first started trying to discuss.

Not What I Did, but How You Reacted

This happens when one person blames their partner for doing something hurtful, but in response, the partner instead blames their spouse's *reaction* for all the trouble. For example, Grace reacted to Mike, saying: "You laughed when I told you that you'd hurt my feelings. I tried to tell you that what you said hurt, but you just made a big joke of it."

"Yes, what you said was so silly and you couldn't laugh about it, so what did you do? You flew off the handle and got all upset and mad at me. One moment you were fine with me and the next I was the bad guy."

Mike tried to say that it was Grace's reaction to his words that was the problem, and not what he actually said. If she had not reacted so emotionally, they wouldn't have had a problem. Or so he thinks.

Great Leaps over All That Is Good

When we are consumed with anger, our minds become Superman or Superwoman—we make great leaps over all the good that is in our spouse and land on their weaknesses. With a magnifying glass in hand, we review all that is wrong with them. We not only notice it, but we mull it over.

Couples may go so far as to wonder why they ever got married in the first place. A husband or wife, according to this distorted view, becomes the meanest, most insensitive, disrespectful person alive. Out spill the ugly words: "You are bad, mean, sick, and you'll never change. Why did I ever think I loved you?" In these moments it's hard to recall anything that was, in the beginning, wonderful or good or attractive about a spouse.

ENDING THE DANGEROUS CYCLE

The pursue-withdraw cycle—in whatever form it takes—is at the core of nearly every fight, no matter what the topic. This cycle keeps couples hurt, distant, and emotionally disconnected. And the cycle is dangerous to marriages when spouses become rigid and are unable to find their way out. The cycle becomes a spin cycle when spouses react too quickly and their patterns of fighting become absorbing and self-perpetuating.

How can you stop where you are, turn toward your partner, and begin again? Undoing the hurt and disconnection may seem impossible at the moment. Maybe for now the two of you are unable to come together and say, "Hey, I don't like this! Can't we start doing this differently? I really want to understand how you feel about our situation. And I do long for you to understand and respect my point of view. I still value you."

Fortunately, when we learn to look at relationships through the lens of connectedness, when we understand the importance of being attached to one another, then our frustrating behaviors and unkind words start to make sense. We see our partners in ways that we've never seen them before. We begin to understand a husband's longing to be emotionally accessible and responsive. We begin to see a wife's yearning for closeness.

The various cycles of pursuing and withdrawing are among the most common and tragic reasons that married couples emotionally disconnect. They are a central problem in troubled marriages. And only as you and your spouse begin to understand your own emotions, and to listen to each other's heart cry, can you begin to find hope, healing, and the beginnings of a safe haven marriage. We'll talk about understanding our emotions in the next chapter.

REFLECTION QUESTIONS

1. What is your experience when you sense the start of an argument? Do you withdraw, freeze, pursue, tend and care, or do you feel safe and securely connected most of the time? What emotions rise up in you?

2. To get a picture of the cycle inside your arguments, think through the following questions regarding a typical fight and then fill out the chart below. How do you respond at first? What does your spouse do then? What do you do next? How do your fights end? How do you and your spouse reconnect emotionally?

Our fights start when_____.

I respond by_____ , then you _____.

I then _____and you then_____.

Our fights end by _____.

We come together and emotionally connect by _____

_____.

3. Think back to your last several arguments. What did you hope would be the outcome? What did *you* hope your spouse would realize, understand, do, or stop doing? What did *your spouse* hope you would realize, understand, do, or stop doing?

4. How rigid is your interactional cycle? Are you able to pull back when in the middle of your cycle and talk to your spouse about *how* you are arguing, not just *what* you are arguing about?

Chapter 7

DEALING WITH
MARITAL EMOTIONS

It isn't that emotions are better than reason, or that feelings say more than words. But, as neuroscience suggests, the expression of emotion and the use of reason are each [intertwined].

—MARY WYLIE AND RICHARD SIMON

Gwen lay on a towel at the beach. The sun was warm and sedating; the waves, lapping nearby, soothed her soul. David, her husband, sat next to her, occasionally stroking her arm. What more could either of them want on a lazy Saturday afternoon?

Then it happened. An attractive young woman strolled by and innocently smiled at them. David made a remark about how slim the young woman was, and the rest of the day was ruined. At least that's what they reported to me the following Tuesday morning as they shared the incident with me (Sharon).

"He makes this really hurtful comment, knowing how sensitive I am about my weight, then he lets me go off by myself," Gwen cried.

"Well, yes, you folded your arms, rolled your eyes, and said I was a jerk. Then you stormed off in a huff. You were clearly mad at me for my innocent remark and wanted to get away from me. And the truth is, I don't know what I did wrong."

"David. Get a grip. You weren't even interested in my feelings. You just stretched out on the towel and fell asleep."

113

"What was I supposed to do? You were clearly mad. You obviously didn't want to be with me. Nothing was going to soothe you. So I let you be."

"You were mad and hurt. Is that right, Gwen?" I interjected, trying to get them to focus on their deeper emotions at the time. "You got up and walked away, but under your ruffled feathers you really longed for something else. It wasn't just about the girl, was it? Is it that you longed for him to show his acceptance of *you?* Didn't you want him to come close?"

"Yes, that's right!" Gwen turned to David. "*I wanted you to follow me.* I knew that the girl who walked by wasn't really a big deal to you. But I wanted you to come up behind me and say, 'I love you, and you are very beautiful to me. I didn't mean to hurt you. Come and sit down with me.' That would have been so powerful. It would have calmed me and let me know that you care about my feelings. And that is all I want from you anyway—to know that you care about how I feel."

David rolled his eyes. "You have got to be kidding! How was I supposed to know? Why didn't you just tell me that instead of walking off in a huff? Then I could've shown you that I value you and care about your feelings. But, Gwen, I've got to tell you something—it's pretty hard to hold you when you have so many thorns!"

WHAT IN THE WORLD ARE EMOTIONS FOR?

Why does an emotion like anger well up inside us when we are actually feeling something else, something like hurt or sadness? Why do we push our spouse away when we really long for him to draw closer to us? And when we get ourselves stuck in a strong emotion like anger, why is it so difficult to move back to the sadness and loneliness that lie behind the anger?

Emotions—and how we understand and deal with them—are essential to making our marriage a safe haven. They are vitally important to our making and maintaining close relationships. Emotions are the winds that drive every couple's cycles of interaction. Emotions direct and fuel the way husbands and wives relate to one another. In a very real sense, our emotions determine whether we stay connected or disconnected, whether we live in a state of harmony or pain.

God's Purpose for Emotions

Many people fail to realize that there is a basic "wisdom" in all of the emotions. They are neither random nor unpredictable. Whatever you're feeling, you're feeling it for a reason! Emotions are the stuff of which life is made—happiness and sadness, elation and depression. As Ecclesiastes 3:4 tells us, there is "a time to weep and a time to laugh, a time to mourn and a time to dance." Because emotions—which we sometimes call "feelings"—are God-given, they are designed into us to serve a purpose. God created us as feeling women and men.

Emotions are biologically based and are a synthesis of all that you experience at any particular time. Your brain processes all the information perceived by your senses and converts that information into emotions. You do not have an experience or a thought without an accompanying emotion. Some of these emotions may be imperceptible, but they are there nevertheless. Emotions are intertwined with your beliefs, expectations, thoughts, and with every experience.

Your emotions help you make sense of the world around you and provide your experiences with meaning. Emotions also make you aware of your deeper needs, such as the need for significance, purpose, meaning, and mastery. And in marriage, emotions are built-in responses that signal when there is a disconnection in your relationship; thus they can help reconnect you and your spouse. Most important, emotions cue you to your need for closeness, love, acceptance, comfort, respect, and understanding in your relationship with your spouse.

Five Ways Emotions Affect Us

Emotions serve five essential purposes in our lives. Let's consider those purposes. To illustrate their function, we'll use sadness as an example:

1. Emotions tell us that we have a need. Sadness, for example, lets us know that we have lost something valuable and need to be comforted. It also makes us sensitive to any sign that our need may not be met, such as distancing or rejection by our spouse.

2. Emotions direct our thoughts. Because we feel sad, all through the day our minds go back to our loss. We may think about how sad we are, or that we are alone in our sadness. We might go over in our minds how wrong our spouse was and whether we should trust him again. Along with every emotion there are thoughts about others, about ourselves, and about the emotional safety of our relationships.

3. Emotions give meaning to our thoughts—and not necessarily an accurate meaning. Sadness might tell us, however erroneously, "I deserve to be alone and sad. I'm sad and alone because I'm unlovable." Or it might tell us, rightly, "I keep criticizing my spouse, and it's hurting our marriage."

4. Emotions prompt us to respond. "Maybe I'll take a chance and try to talk with my spouse." Or, "I'm feeling so bad, I don't want to talk to anybody. I'll just withdraw for a while and pull away from others." Intense emotions tend to override other cues. When hurt by your spouse, all you can focus on is your hurt. Intense emotions also trigger strong (and cyclical) behavioral responses like pursuing and withdrawing.

5. Emotions inspire responses from others. They literally instruct others in how to respond to us. Suppose your spouse notices that you're walking around the house with a downcast face. He might say, "I see that you are sad; let me comfort you." On the other hand, he may remark, "All day you've sulked and ignored me, and I'm fed up with your bad moods!"

Sadness, for example, helps us through the grieving process, which is its purpose. Emotions like sadness, anger, guilt, and fear—and the natural responses that follow them—are all innate, God-designed processes in all of us. That's the good news. The bad news is that we don't always use our emotions the way God intended!

WHAT HAS HAPPENED TO OUR EMOTIONS?

In a perfect world, in a perfect marriage, you and your spouse would be perfectly attuned to what the other is sensing and feeling. You would be able to acknowledge your emotions, expressing them in such a way as to elicit a connecting response from one another. Unfortunately, that is usually not what happens. Your imperfect humanness, your individual personality, your culture, your genetics, how you were raised to understand and utilize your emotions, experiences in past relationships, and your ability to hurt and to remember and hold on to hurts—all these elements affect the way you express and regulate your emotions. These factors all contribute to your emotions losing their natural, adaptive purpose.

To better understand how to handle your emotions in marriage, it can be helpful to think of emotions as falling into two categories.

Primary Emotions

Primary emotions are the healthy, core feelings we have at any particular moment. They are adaptive; these emotions have a mission to accomplish. As we've seen, the emotion of sadness arises when we've lost something precious. We experience anger when our rights have been violated. Fear raises its head when we are threatened, and guilt when we have violated a rule. These all serve a purpose. They are necessary to life itself, and useful and productive if we understand and make sense of them. Studies have shown that the common primary emotions felt by all people across all cultures are anger, fear, surprise, hurt/distress, shame, sadness/despair, joy, love, and pain.

Secondary Emotions

Secondary emotions are reactions and attempts to manage our primary emotions. They occur when we feel overwhelmed or aren't quite sure what we're really feeling is safe. For instance, instead of sharing your wife's sadness over the loss of her wedding ring, you get angry at her for swimming with the ring on her finger. You tell her that anyone with common sense wouldn't swim in the ocean wearing a wedding ring. Anger helps you manage your sadness. It is easier to be angry than it is to cope with the loss.

Sometimes anger is our primary emotion, especially as a response to a violation of injustice. Because we are overwhelmed by anger or believe that anger is "wrong" and destructive, we often don't express it or stand up for ourselves. Instead, we become anxious, numb, explosive, compliant, or fearful.

When we habitually rely on secondary emotions, we lose touch with our primary feelings and don't know how to express them. Secondary emotions are usually anger ("reactive" anger, which is not the same as primary anger), frustration, anxiety, resentment, and guilt. We express them by:

- Being critical and blaming
- Justifying and defending ourselves
- Masking what we usually feel through addictions, workaholism, busyness, or distracting activities such as television and computer games
- Stuffing feelings and numbing ourselves to certain emotions

Switching back and forth from feeling one emotion to another: anger, then sadness, fear, then anger again. During this process, you come close to others, then pull away, then fear being disconnected, then attempt to come close again.

Instead of reaching for your spouse when you are sad, you manage your need for closeness by getting angry and blaming. It is as though you get your emotional wires crossed. The "need-for-closeness-and-understanding" wire gets crossed with your "need-for-distance" wire. Often, the longing for intimacy gets crossed with your frustration, and at the very moment you most long to be close, instead you find yourself pushing away. Likewise, when your spouse needs you the most, you freeze and become cold because intimacy feels too vulnerable.

Trying to be less emotional or more logical never really gets you out of the confusion. The direct path from "I'm hurt and I need you" to "I'll ask you to comfort me" is often obstructed. It ends up like this:

"I'm hurt but I won't tell you—instead I'll pull away and maybe even explode."

Or, "I am embarrassed and feel self-conscious, so I'll get angry and criticize you."

Or, "I feel afraid that you might leave if you know how I really feel, so I'll push you away."

Or, "I feel alone, so I'll blame you for the way I feel."

Needless to say, this style of relating does not, cannot, and will not create a safe haven. Instead, it leads to emotional disconnection that may last for hours, days, or even weeks.

Remember in earlier chapters, how we identified the roles of "withdrawer" and "pursuer"? Look how connected these roles are to secondary emotions.

Although the "pursuing" spouse expresses anger, frustration, anxiety, and fear through attacking, criticizing, and blaming, those efforts usually disguise feelings of panic, insecurity, fear of abandonment, rejection, and loss of worth. The silence or pulling away of the other spouse is not only frustrating and maddening, but also frightening—it feels like rejection. So the pursuer is fighting against a sense of loss, a sense of being pushed away.

Meanwhile, the "withdrawing" spouse usually defends his position and feels frustration and often anger. But underneath secondary emotions he is often feeling intimidated, incompetent, and unable to please his spouse. Withdrawers often feel a paralyzing helplessness, convinced that no matter what they do it won't change the situation. The constant criticism and pursuit of their spouse feels like an attack, and their natural response is to protect themselves and get as far away from the attack as possible. They feel they will never be able to live up to the standards and expectations of their pursuing spouse, and their efforts will fail to calm and please their spouse.

When Secondary Emotions Become "Absorbing States"

An emotional state is "absorbing," as the label implies, when we cannot put it aside. It takes control and absorbs all our energy and thought. When we are in the grip of one emotional state, it is difficult to imagine experiencing another emotion.

Do you remember a time when you were angry with your spouse for something she did? Your heart pounded, your thoughts raced, and all you could think of was, *How could she do that to me?* As the withdrawer, you attempted to defend yourself, telling your spouse how wrong she was for coming to that particular conclusion about you. But the more you defended yourself, trying to prove that you weren't as bad as she made you out to be, the more frustrated you became. You sensed that you were not going to change your wife's opinion, and so your sense of helplessness, resignation, and desire to pull away took over. You recoiled, shut down, and let the waves roll off your back.

As the *pursuing* spouse, your secondary emotions of anger, hurt, and frustration consumed you, and from that position you approached your husband. You felt you were justified in pointing out that his behavior made you feel uncared for or that he forgot to do something that makes the household run smoothly. You felt that if you didn't pursue him and express your concerns, he would never do what you ask, never see the injustice in his actions, never understand how hurt you feel. So, in anger, you pursued him. And, as far as you're concerned, the things you did and said were both appropriate and right.

John Gottman found that in distressed couples, negative emotions take over and consume one, if not both, partners. Intense emotions such as anger, frustration, or resentment have the power to override all other feelings. The central area of our brain is triggered and shouts the message "Danger ahead!" All sorts of alarms go off in our body. These signals, or warnings, are so strong that they shut out all other systems, including kindness, understanding, thoughtfulness, and compassion. We begin making our case or defending our position. And a negative, rigid cycle is set in motion—a cycle that destroys, at least for a time, any emotional connectedness between a husband and wife.

THE THORNS AND THE ROSE

"Your spouse is like a rosebush," I (Sharon) said in desperation one day as I sat with Jeff and Marissa in my office, "and you're both focusing on each other's thorny stems instead of your tender roots." They had bickered all the way through the session, and neither of them seemed even remotely aware that their cold, attacking words masked a deep longing for tenderness in their hearts.

Jeff and Marissa's marital problems surfaced when Jeff's company transferred him to a different office, which was located an hour and a half away from their home. This required Jeff to leave early in the morning and return home well after dinnertime. It left Marissa home alone to care for the kids and all the household responsibilities.

By the time they got in to see me, she was fuming. "You just go on your merry way to work in the morning, and you're back just in time to kiss the kids good night, and then you park yourself in front of the television. You don't help me a bit, even though I've told you that I'm completely overloaded. Don't you care about all the pressure I'm under? I am mad and so resentful that you took on this job!"

Jeff shook his head. "We've been through this a thousand times. Of course I help you when I can. But you explode at everything I do. I've got plenty of pressure at work, trying to learn a new job, and I don't need this."

Their ugly cycle was unmistakable—she pursued; he withdrew. All Jeff could see was Marissa's anger, resentment, and frustration. All Marissa could see was Jeff's defensiveness, his cold shoulder, and the back of his head as he fled from the room. Neither could imagine what lay beyond the other's anger, frustration, and defensiveness.

"What do you see when you look at a rosebush?" I asked them. "You see the leaves, stems, and yes, you are very aware of the thorns, especially when you try to smell a rose or pick one. The same thing happens when you look at each other—all you see are the thorns! All you see are your hot emotions: Marissa's anger and resentment, and Jeff's defensiveness and distancing."

I went on to explain that the thorny emotions they readily see in each other are merely a display of their secondary emotions. These emotions are usually prickly and hard. They cause those around us to become defensive or to fight. Secondary emotions do not draw couples together. Just as the thorns on a rose stem protect the rose from predators, so thorny emotions serve to protect husbands and wives against being hurt.

When Jeff saw Marissa's reaction to his new job, he was aware only of her anger. And what was he supposed to do? What would any spouse do with an angry, resentful, rejecting, and explosive partner? He certainly didn't feel like cozying up to her. All he could see was her thorny and protective stem. Naturally, he withdrew.

"When I listen to her criticisms," he told me, "I get frustrated. I push her away and shut her out. She doesn't feel like a teammate."

Jeff was reacting to Marissa's thorny emotions with his own thorny emotions. He told his wife she was selfish, emotional, and that he had shut her out the first week he started his new job.

All this time, in the soil of Marissa's heart were growing tender, succulent roots containing her longings, needs, and softer emotions. These "primary" emotions are at her core, and therefore they are more vulnerable. They are the attachment longings of the heart, the feelings that really matter. That's why I call them "root" emotions.

At the same time, deep in his heart, Jeff is very hurt. He feels he is constantly in the doghouse and nothing he can do will get him out. He feels alone, rejected, incompetent, and fearful of Marissa's unbridled anger. We were able to determine that Jeff was reluctant to express his tender root emotions because he was afraid of Marissa's reaction—he assumed she would attack him in his vulnerability and wound him even more.

Somehow, he found the courage to acknowledge his primary root emotions. He was able to turn to Marissa and say, "I am tired of always feeling worthless, like I am not good enough for you. Yes, I know I haven't been there for you like I should have been. But I just can't come close to you when you criticize me so much. All your words and criticisms are really hurtful. I know this job is tough for us. And I'm not Superman—I'm just me. All I know is, I need your support. I need to feel close to you again."

Marissa was surprised and touched by Jeff's words. She admitted that she'd never wanted to hurt him and that all along she had only wanted to be closer to him. "I feel panicky when you pull away from me and focus exclusively on your work," she told him. "I feel so alone, and I'm afraid you're going to build a whole new life without me and we'll grow apart. I guess I really miss you when you're gone. You've always refueled me, and nowadays you're just not around long enough for us to connect. You're so important to me—and I really look forward to your coming home."

Jeff's mouth dropped open. He couldn't believe that despite all Marissa's outbursts, she sincerely longed for his companionship. "Jeff," I asked him, "can you hold on to Marissa's root emotions and longings? Can you stop reacting to her thorns and instead imagine gliding your hand down the stem into the sandy soil beneath and reach for her heart?"

The effect on Jeff was quite stunning. "Yes," he said, his voice choked with emotion. "I can do that. The thought of having to argue and convince Marissa of my love and dedication seems impossible. I can't come close when she is so critical and blaming. But, yes, I think I can comfort her loneliness and fears. If she really wants me to, I'll be there for her no matter what."

THE M&M COATING

Remember the scene on the beach, when David offended Gwen by making a comment about another woman? Let's take a second look at that situation. Why would Gwen want to withdraw her heart from David? There were several reasons. First, she was afraid that David found her unattractive and perhaps even unlovable. Second, she felt devalued when she saw him looking at someone else. Finally, she felt shut out when he didn't understand why she felt the way she did, when he laughed and told her not to be so immature.

Gwen was afraid to express her true feelings—she imagined that if she did, she would feel diminished as a person. Like Gwen, we often avoid certain emotions because we imagine that they indicate some kind of weakness. Other times we fear that if we express a primary emotion, we will lose control. Gwen doesn't want David to see her shame or hurt.

Immediately, Gwen's attachment style clicks in and tells her how to respond in situations like this. Growing up, for example, she was not allowed to express anger directly at her parents. They would scold her and say, "Don't you lose your temper, young lady! How dare you get angry! Go to your room!"

"At home growing up," Gwen explained to me, "I was always told that I was too emotional. Dad never found the time to get to know me, and when I revealed any emotion, he would discipline me for being disrespectful. Nobody would listen to me, so my emotions would swim inside of me, churning with no way to come out except when I got mad." Gwen had learned to use anger in order to be seen, heard, and understood.

So what was Gwen *really* feeling inside right before she got in a huff with David? What were her primary emotions? Here's what she told me.

"What he said just triggered something. I'm sensitive about my body, so any comment that might relate to my size is like a trip switch. I felt hurt, like my stomach turned upside down."

"What's it like, Gwen, to feel your stomach churn like that?" I probed.

"It feels like my whole world is turning upside down. Like the man I love and trust is gone, and in his place is someone who won't protect me or take care of me. David now becomes the enemy. I have to protect myself so he can't hurt me anymore."

"So when you heard David say, 'Get over it, you're just overreacting,' you felt like he was no longer your husband who would protect you, but just a man who, at the drop of a dime, would leave you out on your own. The thought of David leaving and you going through life all alone is terrifying, isn't it?"

"You'd better believe it! The thought of David leaving me is very scary. And it only gets worse when I think he's looking at other attractive women. But he refuses to see it."

"Is it hard for you to share exactly what you've just told me with David? Is it easier to just get mad and push him away before he pushes you away?"

Suddenly David interrupted. "Hey, I get it! Her anger is just like the coating on an M&M. She's mad, but underneath she's soft and afraid. She's scared that I think she's unattractive and that I'm going to leave her. She's actually really hurt and frightened, and her anger is her candy coating. Hey, I can handle that candy coating if I know what is underneath. I want to be close to her. I really do. But her bitterness and her habit of cutting me down as a person— telling me how bad I am—that I can't handle. I run from that!"

At that point we were all moved to tears. David got the message. He'll never be the same again, nor will Gwen. And neither will their marriage.

The question is, How can we learn to share our emotions and longings in ways that our spouse can respond to warmly and receptively? To be able to do this is not manipulative or coercive. It means being true to ourselves and being honest about our deepest feelings. To use the M&M analogy again, it means not focusing on the hard, crunchy coating, but on the heartfelt, softer core inside. This kind of sensitivity toward one another is what building a safe haven marriage is all about, and we need to develop it. But first we need to remove some obstacles.

DISMANTLING EMOTIONAL BLOCKS

There are many emotional blocks that hinder us from acknowledging and feeling our primary emotions. Couples often don't know how to respond to their partners in ways that will elicit positive responses, allowing one another to be emotionally available and responsive. Here are some of the reasons.

No Permission to Feel

Sometimes spouses believe that certain emotions are unacceptable, inappropriate, and dangerous. A husband might say, "Men aren't supposed to need the touchy-feely stuff. Asking for a hug is a weakness. It's effeminate." Perhaps his father did not respect such feelings, or his mother brushed his affectionate efforts aside. The way parents raise a child can set in place automatic self-criticism later in life.

A man might assume that his feelings of sadness are inappropriate and a sign of weakness—"Stop acting like a baby," his mother reminded him whenever he cried—so he fends off his tears by adopting an attitude of indifference and saying, "It's no big deal." Later on, when a situation deeply saddens him, he won't be quite sure what to feel, so he will be numb, or even angry. After a while, it is difficult for him to experience sadness. To make matters worse, it is also difficult for him to comfort his spouse when she experiences sadness or other difficult emotions. He automatically moves away from her, saying, "Look, if you're going to get emotional, then this conversation is over."

Fear of the Emotion Itself

Maybe you've found yourself thinking, *I can't let myself feel that way. I'll cry forever if I get in touch with the sadness.* Or, *I'll lose control and really get angry. Then I'll find out that I'm unlovable.* There is a place of grief, anger, fear, shame, and loneliness inside each of us, a painful core that seems too dangerous to touch. Fear makes us reluctant to explore a place where grief is hidden.

A Sense of Helplessness

This misconception says, "Things will get even worse if I let you know how I feel!" Sometimes a husband avoids expressing a particular emotion because he fears that sharing it with his wife will do more harm than good. Sometimes a wife is afraid that expressing her real feelings will start a fight, escalate an argument, or hurt her husband's feelings. Maybe the husband believes that his wife won't understand him and won't be willing to sit and listen to his feelings. Maybe the wife fears her husband will overreact, get angry, be defensive, criticize her, blame her, or belittle what she says. So both of them stuff their feelings, keep them a secret, or share them with someone else less threatening. Maybe it's like this:

- You don't say anything when you lose a business deal because you fear your wife might start panicking about the finances.
- You don't share how bored you feel on weekends for fear your husband will take it personally.
- You don't express your anger when your wife yells at you for using the bath towels to dry your car, because you don't want to start an argument.
- You don't share how hurt you feel about what your husband said last night, because you assume he'll either be defensive or brush you off as an annoyance.
- You don't ask for help with the children because you fear it will only confirm your wife's already shaky trust in your ability to care for them on your own.
- You apologize and agree to do something your husband's way to end the fight that seems to be going nowhere and has already ruined your Saturday night.
- You say nothing when your wife calls and asks you to pick up dinner on the way home, even though you are tired and longing for a home-cooked meal. You've learned that if you complain, she will say, "You're so selfish! I'm tired, too, you know."

Husbands and wives do it all the time—they stop a fight, de-escalate an argument, and reduce the risk of a partner's exploding, lecturing, crying, or getting mad. But a part of each one goes unseen and not understood. Meanwhile, they assume, "It's safer this way." Still, deep down inside, there is part of each one that feels terribly alone.

REGULATED AND UNREGULATED EMOTIONS

Attachment isn't just about relationships; it is also about learning how to regulate our emotions. It is in the context of relationships that we learn how to view ourselves, how to get our needs met, how to obtain the attention of others, and how to be nurtured and cared for. The four attachment styles outline the four different ways we understand, utilize, and express our emotions.

Those with a *secure attachment style* are comfortable and content within relationships. They aren't afraid to feel the full spectrum of their emotions and are able to express them in ways that are beneficial and productive.

Those with an *anxious attachment style* are concerned with whether they will be loved as they long to be loved. So they experience a spectrum of feelings. They tend to be on an emotional roller coaster and underregulate their emotions.

Those with an *avoidant attachment style* avoid certain emotions that will trigger their attachment system and longings and so make less of or dismiss them. Those with a *fearful attachment style* are also uncomfortable with feelings, as they are scarred by the intense pain that their longings ignite. In both cases, they are likely to hold back emotions, neutralizing them so as not to feel them.

"I am even-keeled, constantly in the same mood," a husband boasted. But actually he was overregulating his emotions, putting the brakes on so as not to feel too much. When we reject or neutralize our emotions, of course, we are denying ourselves the fullness of life that Jesus Christ came to give us. Our emotions are not our enemies. They are useful guides, and they can deepen our relationships and experiences.

But perhaps you are faced with a different situation. Maybe you are unable to regulate your emotions. What you feel, you express, then and there. You go with your feelings even though your emotions are leading you many directions at once and changing directions frequently. You feel you have the right to let out your emotions regardless of the impact on others. You are unable to soothe yourself when you are hurt or angry. Like a bull in a china shop, your emotions wreak havoc on your relationships. As one wife said, "When I feel angry, I let him know how he has made me angry. What am I supposed to do? Not feel? Let him get away with what he has done?"

A good goal is to find ourselves somewhere between those who overregulate and those who underregulate their feelings. As we seek to build a safe haven marriage, we need to work with our spouse so we are both able to access and acknowledge our primary emotions, and to express them in healthy and adaptive ways.

EXPANDING YOUR EMOTIONAL BASE

When each partner is able to access what the other is feeling and needing, a deeper and more complete understanding of each other's genuine longings and needs emerges, along with the capacity to respond to these needs. This is called expanding your emotional base.

The goal for you and your spouse is not only to learn how to express emotions such as anger, but also to expand your awareness and expression of the emotions that lie *beneath* your anger and to express those feelings in new ways—things like sadness, fear of being alone, and fear of being disapproved.

In this way you should be able to say, "I know I was angry that you didn't call me when you should have. I was angry because I felt like you didn't care about me. But I was also worried that something had happened to you. I really needed you tonight, so when I didn't hear from you, I felt both hurt and worried."

From here a couple can find a more secure way of reconnecting around the spouse's worry and hurt, rather than only around her anger. In this way, one spouse is not simply seen as an angry, critical person. Instead, she is seen as angry over a broken agreement, but also as a hurting, worried, frightened loved one who longs for connection. Learning to understand your spouse's feelings, as well as your own, clearly requires both understanding and sensitivity. Following are some important ways we can increase our emotional awareness.

Acknowledge Differing Emotional Temperatures

Each of us comes into marriage with different emotional temperature settings, or comfort levels. For example, Andrew's emotional thermostat setting is actually reflected by his preferred room temperature setting: He is cool, calm, and collected, with well-controlled emotions. His view is, "Why be emotional when you can be logical?"

But alas, he married Bethany, who likes the emotional thermostat set a lot higher. She enjoys a good, heated discussion. She wears her emotions on her sleeve. When she is happy, everyone knows it. When she's mad, well, what you see is what you get.

When they first met, Bethany's open nature attracted Andrew. He saw that she was alive and vibrant. And Bethany was drawn to Andrew as a stable anchor, steady and secure in his feelings. But now their different emotional thermostat settings are causing problems. To Andrew, Bethany's outbursts demonstrate how hopelessly illogical she is. She, in turn, thinks that his reliance on logic is repressive and cold-hearted.

What can a couple do about this kind of a difference?

Emotions are not jumping beans that need to be let out so they can bounce around the room or be stuffed in a box with the lid tightly shut. Nor should you and your spouse battle over which emotional setting is more productive: hot or cool. Instead, emotions are to be understood and expressed with respect and then used as information and energy to move us toward each other and into a more balanced, healthy marriage.

Respect the Way Your Spouse Feels and Expresses Emotions

Some couples have a more avoidant style of relating and may appear to blunt, defuse, or deflect both positive and negative feelings. They come across as being cool and collected. But this doesn't mean that they feel their emotions less deeply than more emotive types. When you hook up these nonexpressive spouses to physiological instruments and then engage them in an argument, they show all the signs of high emotional arousal. After a fight it may seem that the emotional water just rolls off their backs, but this isn't so. They continue to be aroused long after a fight ends. It takes time for their physiological measures to come down. Emotional suppression does not make them immune to emotional pain—a point that women should keep in mind, since men are often more emotionally suppressed.

In counseling, wives often describe their husbands as "unable to feel" or "cool and chilly." These supposedly inexpressive males live behind a shield of protection. They have learned to guard their hearts and are convinced that being emotional is for women. They pride themselves on their emotional flat-line.

One wife told me that her husband "is incapable of feeling anything. He just doesn't have the brain cells to process feelings on a deep level."

I (Sharon) turned to her husband and asked him, "Is that true? Does it hurt when she says that?"

His eyes dropped toward the floor for a moment. Then with tears welling up in his eyes, he answered very slowly, "Yes, of course it hurts. Her words hurt deeply. I've just learned how not to let the hurt show!"

"What are the tears for?" I asked quietly.

"Well, she always tells me that I am aloof and cold, and that I am a failure as a husband. It is very sad. And I don't know what to do."

At this point, the wife's eyes widened in disbelief. She simply shook her head and said, "I have no idea where *that* came from! He sure doesn't talk about his feelings at home."

Search for Your Primary Emotions

If you are not able to do so *during* an argument, then immediately *after* an argument, pause and try to figure out what you were actually feeling. Were you defensive because your spouse hurt your feelings? Were you blaming because you felt your spouse was devaluing you? Did you react to your spouse's defensiveness instead of trying to understand why he needed to be defensive? What were your root emotions, and what were your spouse's? Don't get caught in the details of the argument. Instead, look inside and honestly examine your experience.

Focus on Feelings Rather Than Details

Fighting over who did what in the event is senseless. Instead, pause. Then start over. Go back and talk through why it seemed to make sense for you to defend yourself, or why it seemed to make sense for your wife to criticize you or to come on so strong. Maybe you felt blamed and incompetent. Maybe she felt overwhelmed by all she has to do. Be determined to get past your destructive relational habits and to find out what is going on inside. By being understanding, you can soothe each other, calm troubled feelings, and restore peace. Then you will be able to come together and problem-solve, finding ways to do things differently the next time.

Express Your Feelings

Not being honest about feelings can cause havoc in your relationship. Maybe your wife asks you what the matter is. You know what's wrong— you're in a bad mood and just can't seem to shake it. Maybe you're still hurt and mad over the argument earlier that day. But you tell her that nothing is wrong, that she should not be so sensitive, or maybe you growl, "Just leave me alone!"

Perhaps your husband asks where you want to go to dinner, and you say, "It doesn't matter." So he decides on an Italian restaurant. You don't feel like eating Italian food, but you don't have a better idea, so you say nothing. But as you drive along in silence, you begin to think about how many times you have sacrificed for him and how he never considers your wishes and wants. You shut down and close up.

In your attempt to avoid conflict by not sharing your thoughts, needs, desires, and feelings, you actually don't avoid conflict at all. Your spouse senses your refusal to speak the truth, your avoidance of voicing your opinions, or your easygoing "whatever" and interprets it as a lack of caring on your part. His attachment system is triggered, and he reacts by getting angry, criticizing your character, or complaining about your behavior. Or maybe he simply shuts down. Either way, the result is emotional disconnection.

Use Self-Control When Expressing Emotions

It is unhealthy to be dishonest about your feelings, or to stuff them, or to refuse to communicate them. But sharing your feelings in an unmanaged, unregulated, almost untamed way can be just as damaging. When you give yourself permission to overreact, saying, "This is what I feel and I'm going to let it all hang out!" you fail to take responsibility for the way your outburst will affect your spouse and your relationship. Nor does the excuse "I just can't seem to stop myself when I'm in the moment" justify the hurt that is caused. Our emotions fuel our words, and the Bible speaks of that in no uncertain terms: "The tongue . . . is a fire, a world of evil among the parts of the body. It corrupts the whole person, sets the whole course of his life on fire, and is itself set on fire by hell. All kinds of animals, birds, reptiles and creatures of the sea are being tamed and have been tamed by man, but no man can tame the tongue. It is a restless evil, full of deadly poison" (James 3:6–8).

Regulating emotions doesn't mean refusing to feel. It means having self-control over the way we express our emotions, and that self-control is essential to the health of every marital relationship. Of course you are entitled to your emotional experience. Your emotions give you information about your environment and signal when things aren't right. But allowing your emotions to be expressed in a way that is damaging to your spouse is harmful and foolish.

Wisely regulated emotions are indispensable to drawing close and remaining connected with your spouse. Pause when you feel your emotions welling up inside you. Take a moment or two to understand what emotions you are feeling, and think about how you are about to express them. Exploding will not accomplish what your heart longs for. Instead, it will injure your spouse and your relationship.

Don't Let Your Spouse's Emotions Overwhelm You

Bob felt weighed down by Kathy's emotions. He didn't know what to do with all her needs, desires, and feelings. He longed to understand her and let her know that he cared. But sometimes she was just too much for him, and he didn't feel safe enough to express how he felt.

"So I filter her out when she is talking," he explained to me. "I lower the volume in my mind when she comes after me with overheated emotions. It's impossible for me to listen to her words and to sift through all that she is throwing at me. At those times I have three options: I can go into work mode, I can offer her a solution, or I can just filter her out."

I explained to Bob that we tend to push away emotions we can't tolerate within ourselves. "It may be that she's bringing up feelings you're not comfortable with. But try to find out what she wants the most."

So Bob asked Kathy, "What do you need from me? I honestly don't know what to do with your emotions."

She was quiet for a moment and then said, "You can't do anything with my emotions except to listen and try to understand them. I just don't want to be alone in them. I don't need a solution; I just need to be listened to."

The Gentle Art of Listening

In our hectic, clock-driven culture, we have lost our ability to listen. Our world seems to be set on fast-forward, filled with relentless activity. Families seldom gather around the dinner table, and couples rarely have the luxury of sitting quietly at the end of each day, ready to talk and to listen. Returning to the gentle art of listening can be very powerful in fostering a healthy marriage and creating a safe haven.

Gentle listening doesn't mean problem solving, which is a common male strategy. Often men, once they have listened long enough to get the gist of what's wrong, simply offer a solution. Instead of solving the problem, their "solution" either stops an emotion dead in its tracks or makes it a hundred times more intense. On the other hand, true listening does not exacerbate emotion. Listening to emotions seems dangerous. The concern is that if you listen, somehow the emotions will be intensified. Instead, many spouses feel if they ignore, discourage, or solve the problem, then the emotions will go away. Listening is, instead, actually soothing. It feels like support and genuine care. The listened-to spouse feels seen and understood. And the problem begins to dissolve or finds its own solution. The emotions are calmed.

Here are some guidelines that can help us develop the gentle art of listening:

Listen to the heart of your spouse. Give your spouse your full attention. Acknowledge your spouse's feelings with a brief comment: "Really." "Oh." "Mmm."

Name your spouse's feeling or emotional experience. Doing so does not escalate the emotion (make them more mad, angry, or sad); rather, studies have shown that it can be very soothing and comforting. It can de-escalate, defuse, and unravel hurt feelings that might otherwise lead to an argument.

Look beyond your spouse's words and try to determine what emotions lie behind them. Use a word in a sentence that shows your spouse that you understand what she is experiencing. Here are some examples:

"The gas bill is so high this month."

"Oh?"

"You seem to have totally blown off our plans for your getting a part-time job to help out."

"I know you're disappointed that I don't have a job yet. I'm sure that adds to your worry of how we will pay the bills. This is really a tough season for us." (Instead of defending yourself or taking it personally, hold your spouse's feelings.)

"Yes, I know you're trying, and it's not your fault. I'm just so worried about how we are going to make ends meet." (Spouses respond much more healthily when they feel heard and understood.)

• • •

"I got to the bank just as they were closing the doors. Those kids were so hard to deal with in the grocery store, it took me longer than I thought."

"That must have been disappointing." (You need say nothing else. You and your wife both know that the deposit will now be a day late.)

• • •

"Your cell phone kept beeping. I didn't know what to do, so I took the battery out."

"You took the battery out? Why would you do that?"

"I really don't care. You know I am not going to take care of all your business stuff; I have enough of my own things to worry about."

"You sound very hurt and frustrated with me all of a sudden. Sorry if what I said made you defensive. Let me start over. It must have been frustrating for you to hear my phone beep all morning. I am sorry it distracted you from your work." (When you realize you are defending yourself instead of listening and understanding, stop, and start over.)

• • •

Let your spouse feel that you really understand their experience. Instead of repeating back to them what they've already said to you, you can say things like:

"Sounds like a frustrating day."

"You sound angry about what happened."

"That must have been very disappointing."

"You seem really hurt by what was said."

Offer a solution *only* when your spouse asks for one. If you find yourself anxious and eager to problem-solve, criticize, or comment, take a deep breath, relax your body, and start focusing again on listening. Keep reminding yourself about the power of listening, and even if your spouse is telling you all the things that you do wrong, just be still.

Try to understand what is going on inside you when your spouse expresses his emotions. Do you feel you have to question, blame, or micromanage your spouse? Avoid saying such things as, "Well, what do you expect if you get such a late start on your day?" or, "Well, this isn't the first time you have taken what I said and twisted it." It is very difficult for your spouse to share his feelings with you when your words express blame, scrutiny, or control.

You may find yourself feeling overwhelmed by your spouse's emotions. Is she expressing feelings that are difficult and painful for you to feel or even tolerate? Be honest and if necessary say, "You know, I really want to listen to you, but it's hard for me right now. Can we take a break and finish up in an hour or so?"

Express your concerns about the way things are said. Although all feelings are valid, the way we express them is not always acceptable. Most husbands and wives say that it is not *what* their spouse says that hurts or angers them the most, but it is often the *tone of voice* or *body language* that causes the problem. When your spouse says something in a particular way that is hurtful, condescending, or devaluing, instead of withdrawing or attacking back, say something like this: "I really do want to hear your perspective on this situation, but when you use that tone of voice, it feels like you're talking down to me, and that makes me want to pull back or shut down. Can you talk to me without so much volume or anger?" Or, "I would really like to talk about this issue at some point. It makes me angry when you keep turning away when I try to talk to you. How do you suggest we go about talking this over?"

Be open to correction. Take a closer look at yourself. Are you emotionally detached and neutral because it is safer to be that way? Is your lack of responsiveness causing you to miss out on a rich closeness with your spouse? Or if your spouse keeps telling you to tone down your emotions and not to be so angry in your tone and words, then take an honest look at yourself. How do you express your frustration? With anger? Hurt? Consider your tone of voice, your choice of words, and your attitude.

The interchange of love, needs, and longings is primarily done through the channel of emotions. Our attachment system is triggered by and in turn triggers our emotions, and we protest and get angry or defensive in an attempt to gain our spouse's attention and restore the relationship. Our emotions direct the way we interact with our spouse. If we do not learn how to identify our primary emotions, and then regulate them either by expressing them more openly or by calming them down a bit, we can damage our connection with our spouse. That's why it is essential for us to gain a broader understanding of our feelings. In doing so, we find ourselves drawing closer to one another, building trust, compassion, and availability, and moving toward a safe haven marriage.

Reflection Questions

1. How do you deal with and express your emotions? Do you tend to over- or underregulate your emotions? How does your spouse experience the way you express your emotions?

2. Review your last argument with your spouse. What were your root, or primary emotions? What were your thorny, secondary emotions? How did you express them? What did you long for your spouse to understand about you?

3. Are you more of a pursuer or a withdrawer in your marital relationship? What is your emotional experience of that position? How would you like it to be different?

4. What are some areas of emotional growth you'd like to address in yourself? In your marriage and in relating to your spouse?

Part Three

MOVING FROM DISCONNECTION TO A SAFE HAVEN MARRIAGE

Chapter 8

EMOTIONALLY RECONNECTING

Humans' ability to grow is infinite . . . when they feel safe.

—CARL ROGERS

*M*arriage means sharing life together, loving and caring for one another no matter what, until death comes between you. Marriage requires two people to dedicate their lives to working, living, nurturing, understanding, laughing, growing, and exploring alongside one another. Marriage also requires the management of hurt feelings. Marital arguments and fights often revolve around hurts of the heart. A wife feels her husband is emotionally unavailable or inaccessible. A husband perceives his wife to be insensitive when she responds to him. A conversation crosses the line and becomes an argument or fight when one spouse believes his feelings have been overlooked, ignored, or wounded. The hurt spouse begins to feel that her husband is not there for her and does not care about her perspective.

None of us want to live with pain, especially the emotional pain of having been hurt by the person closest to us. As we've seen, when we feel our spouse doesn't value, respect, or understand us, or is emotionally unavailable or unresponsive, our attachment system is triggered. In response, often negative ways

141

of relating get set in motion. This, in turn, leads to emotional disconnection from our spouse.

When disconnection takes place, it becomes difficult for a couple to continue to be involved with each other in areas that touch their hearts. Too often this leads to drifting apart and, eventually, going separate ways. Avoiding the initial disconnection, or quickly repairing it, is essential. And the key to emotionally connecting during and after disagreements is for both spouses to be aware of their emotions, to communicate about them, and to manage them.

Based on early experiences, personality, culture, and other such factors, each of us brings into our marriage a set of relationship expectations and ways of dealing with hurts. We also have an internal view of our own lovability, our spouse's ability and willingness to love us, and ideas about how we can and cannot express our needs and longings. This brings us back to attachment styles.

If you are *securely attached,* you are assured that your spouse loves and cares for you, so you are able to experience and express your emotions readily. Because you feel confident in your relationship, you are able to share your hurts. You also know how to respond in productive and caring ways if and when you hurt, or are hurt by, your spouse.

If you are *anxiously attached,* you always wonder whether your spouse will love you "enough." You have difficulty regulating your emotions; they can be overwhelming. You are afraid of being left alone and not understood; therefore, in order to cope with your hurts, you cling, cry, argue, panic, get angry, or placate. You may also desperately try to keep the peace. You do all this in hopes of preserving the love and connection you crave.

If you are more *avoidantly attached,* you are emotionally controlled and emotionally self-sufficient. Because emotions that touch your softer, tender side are painful, you avoid them in yourself as well as in others. You deal with hurts either by ignoring them, defending against them, or withdrawing in self-protection.

If you are more *fearfully attached,* you are afraid to come close to your spouse because in the past closeness resulted in great pain. So you respond by vacillating: You feel hurts deeply, so you snap back in self-protection. Then, after sufficient time passes, you might reach out for comfort again.

The previous chapter helped us gain a better and deeper understanding of our emotions. We hope that, as you read, you were able to understand the various feelings that lie beneath your marital interactions. It isn't easy to look at oneself and see, as in a mirror, how others experience you. It is especially difficult for husbands and wives to understand how they appear to one another. It requires courage to take responsibility for yourself and to explore the ways you respond when you feel hurt.

In this chapter you will continue to learn how to understand your own emotions and to develop new ways of expressing your feelings to your spouse—a communication style that is less defensive and critical. As you understand yourself better, you will also gain a deeper compassion for and understanding of your spouse. Before long, you both will be safe enough to share your hearts and to ask for closeness and comfort. You will be able to reach out to each other from a position of vulnerability.

This new experience of reaching out, instead of withdrawing or pursuing, becomes the beginning of a new cycle. And this cycle will foster a more secure attachment bond between you and your partner. Your marriage can now become the safe haven you've both dreamed about.

There are three key aspects of changing your interactional pattern, reconnecting your hearts, and fostering a safe haven. First, you need to gain an understanding of the ways you argue, discuss, interact, and react to hurts in your marriage. Second, the withdrawer will need to go through a process in order to reemerge and emotionally reconnect. Third, the pursuer will go through a similar process to soften her approach and emotionally reconnect.[1]

GAINING AN UNDERSTANDING OF YOUR ARGUMENTS

The following steps will make you more aware of how you argue, and help you stop your cycle at the beginning of your argument, before it starts.

Beware of Battling over What Happened

As we've seen, unless you're trying to work toward a solution, fighting over the event or "what happened" during past quarrels typically escalates an argument.

Suppose, for example, that you and your spouse have just set up a home business and are sorting out who needs to report the employees' hours to the accountant. If there has been a problem in the past, of course, going back and seeing where the ball was dropped is of value. But suppose your wife is nursing hurt feelings because she thinks you criticized her for not turning in the hours on time, even though she was unsure it was her responsibility. In that case, reviewing the details and defending each of your positions will only make you both feel more hurt and misunderstood. That is because you are not returning to the argument to seek understanding and to say, "How did I hurt you? I am sorry." And that's what needs to be said. This is key to repairing your bond after a fight.

Jake and Fran know the long-term impact their fights have had on their relationship. When they married, Jake's daughter, Teresa, was eight years old. Now Teresa is grown up and getting married in a few months. For weeks now, Jake and Fran have been fighting. Their arguments revolve around things like what money to spend on the wedding, who to invite, and what the invitations will say.

In the counseling room one day, Jake and Fran were arguing about how the names of the bride's parents should be listed on the invitation. Fran was furious because Jake had made a decision without consulting her. He defended himself by reviewing the details, reminding Fran of the numerous opportunities she had been given to proofread the final copy.

As I (Sharon) listened, I knew that this kind of dialogue would only escalate the problem. Because it was far more important for them to move toward understanding and acceptance, they needed to focus on their primary emotions, I asked them both a question: "I know you are trying to find out who was responsible for the invitations, but what are you *feeling* as you talk about what happened?"

Be Aware When You Are Defending or Blaming

Are you reviewing a past fight with the aim of finding out who was at fault? Or are you trying to understand how your spouse felt? When you sense that you are at the beginning of an argument that is not going to move toward greater understanding or resolve, pause. Take a quick second to think about what you're *saying,* and remain conscious of what you are *doing.* Are you acting or speaking in some inappropriate way because you don't know what to say or how to communicate your feelings? Maybe you feel hurt by what your spouse said. Are you making an angry, sarcastic, or critical remark in response? Does your body language communicate anger when, in fact, you feel pain? Are you defending yourself or blaming your spouse? Are you pointing out to your spouse that she is wrong to feel or react a certain way? Stop. *Slow down!* Perhaps you are beginning your cycle of defending and blaming. Recognize it. Then talk about it with your spouse. If you can't find the words you need, tell your spouse. Ask your partner to help you. Move toward gaining understanding of each other's perspective rather than defending or blaming.

Realize How You Are Talking

When I raised the question about feelings with Jake and Fran, they stopped midsentence and looked at each other. "Well, I guess I am defending myself," Jake admitted.

"Yeah, I feel I am in hot pursuit, trying to be heard," said Fran.

They both confessed that they were so busy arguing their own points, they were unable to hear each other's perspective or to understand what the other was really feeling. Pulling back, admitting to how they were expressing themselves (quick to defend and hot in pursuit), and naming their cycle (defending and blaming) seemed to ease the moment. It gave them space to pull back and share their feelings with each other.

"I must have some strong feelings about my daughter getting married, because I sure have strong opinions about the wedding," Jake said.

"Yes," Fran said with a nod, "I have a strong need to attack you and blame you, so I guess I need to stop and figure out why."

They both agreed that talking more about their inner experiences would help them understand their actions and reactions. One way or another, they needed to come to terms with their daughter's wedding.

Understand Your Feelings As Well As Your Spouse's

It bears repeating: To avoid the emotional disconnection that results from a cycle of withdrawing and pursuing, you'll need to learn how to manage your emotions. Once you can identify and name the primary emotions that lie beneath your secondary feelings, you will feel less angry and critical, or frustrated and withdrawn.

You will also gain a deeper understanding of your spouse's experience. You will begin to recognize what lies beneath your spouse's anger or numbness, and to see your spouse as more than just an angry, critical wife or an uninvolved, uncaring husband. As your understanding grows, so does your ability to express your emotions and ask for your deeper needs to be met. Your compassion and acceptance of your spouse also increases. You are able to change and be changed so that your marriage can grow.

With Jake and Fran, I suggested that we move past the upcoming events and talk more about their emotional experience. I asked Jake and Fran to turn toward each other and share their thoughts and emotions concerning the upcoming wedding. "What does it feel like to watch Teresa get married?" I asked.

Jake took a deep breath and dived in. "I can't help but wonder if I was the best parent I could have been. Did I give Teresa all that she needs to be a wife and a woman? This is very hard for me."

Fran talked frankly about how hard it had been for her to raise Teresa. She recalled the years of custody battles with Teresa's mother, and how she always felt caught in the middle, depicted as the evil stepmother. "I wanted to be involved in Teresa's life. But I was told to stay out. And Jake would always take Teresa's mother's side. I learned to stay out of the way when it came to Teresa."

Jake tried to defend himself by saying, "I never told you to stay out of Teresa's life. That's what you *chose* to do."

"Yes, Jake," Fran interrupted, "because I felt so inadequate and worthless as a stepmother. I just didn't know how to stand up to Teresa's mother when she criticized me. Don't defend yourself, Jake, and don't shut down. I'm not blaming you or saying you're bad or anything else. I'm just telling you how I felt then, and how I feel now. I just need you to listen and try to understand my struggle and pain."

Reach Out Toward Each Other Instead of Blaming or Withdrawing

Jake reached out his hand and placed it on the couch next to Fran. This was his attempt to let Fran know that he was still on track with the conversation, and that he hadn't pulled away. Jake was beginning to understand and accept Fran's experience while understanding his own.

Jake said, "I have been very hurt by you in the past, Fran, but I'm really not angry at you. It is just a shame that it all turned out the way it did. I have a lot of regrets that you and I didn't do things differently. And I admit that I was afraid to stand up to Teresa's mother, mostly because I was afraid to be taken back to court. So I let her run over us both. And since you were always mad at Teresa, I didn't know what to do about it. So I just shut down and withdrew."

Fran looked at Jake and somehow managed to be quiet. There was plenty she could have said, but instead of accusing and criticizing Jake, she moved to a more vulnerable position and said, "I just wanted you to acknowledge that I was a good enough parent. I wanted your support—I still want it. But since I never got it, I was so hurt that I attacked you. I came after you. I might have blamed you during those years, but right now I just want us to be able to understand each other."

Confessing how she dealt with her hurt feelings, Fran then expressed her tender feelings for her husband. "I love you, Jake. I really do. And I feel guilty about always criticizing and being on your back. I mostly regret being bitter about it all. In the long run it has hurt both Teresa and our marriage. The sad thing is, I just didn't know how to do it differently. I am so sorry about it all."

In this way, Jake and Fran were able to turn toward each other and acknowledge each other's experience rather than defend and rationalize it away. As they did this, understanding and empathy for each other grew, and they were able to be a source of comfort to each other.

Respect Each Other's Perspective

When you turn toward your spouse, you are better able to understand his perspective. You are then able to hold in one hand your own feelings, opinions, and needs while holding in your other hand your spouse's perspective and feelings. As you do this, you are better able to respond in a way that is in the best interest of you, your spouse, and the relationship.

Jake and Fran listened to each other and tried not to criticize each other. Even though they were tempted, they refused to debate the events. Instead, they held each other's feelings and empathized. They did not always agree with one another. Yes, they admitted that there were specific times when each of them had failed to be thoughtful, sensitive, or responsive.

But now they were able to come together, taking responsibility for their roles in their family problems. Each apologized for contributing to the hurts, and they both shared their regrets. They began to understand each other's feelings and to express tenderness toward each other. And they both consoled each other in their hurt.

Finally, they were able to team up and say, "How do we want to walk Teresa into her new marriage? And how can we do things differently with Teresa in the years to come?"

Clarification Communication: What Did You Mean by That?

Before being defensive or quick to blame, first gather more information. Clarify what your spouse meant when she said or did something disturbing. As we outlined in chapter 3, clarification communication enables you to understand the intent of your spouse before reacting to what you thought your spouse meant.

At one point, I remember Fran asking, "Jake, can you tell me what you mean by that statement? Because right now I feel like you don't value me as a helpmate. That makes me want to fight for my worthiness and let you know that you have it wrong: I am a capable and worthy person. I don't want to do that, so can you please help me understand what you meant when you said, 'I never like coming home to an uptight woman'?"

And Jake asked for clarification this way: "Fran, when you say, 'What were you thinking when you decided that?' I feel you don't trust me or value my suggestions or input. No matter what I bring up, I feel you shoot it down as wrong. I feel like an idiot. And I am not an idiot. So I want to know what you meant when you said that because I am starting to feel attacked right now, and when I feel attacked, I defend myself by shutting down and ignoring what you say and feel. And I am trying not to do that anymore."

Be Willing to Be Influenced and to Do Things Differently

Jake and Fran had to be willing to short-circuit an argument, to stop defensiveness or blaming in its tracks, and to hold one another's perspective.

Like Jake and Fran, you are being challenged to grow. You need to risk understanding your own emotions and needs. You also need to be open to your spouse's suggestions, and willing to meet your spouse's needs. All this will require you to stretch beyond the typical ways you are accustomed to reacting and responding. You will need to awaken feelings and learn to regulate them. You'll have to find a way to express your emotions, your needs, and your point of view differently. As a withdrawer, it will be important for you to come out from behind your shield and connect with your spouse. As a pursuer, your growing edge will require you to put down your verbal weapons and risk softening your heart and gently connecting with your spouse. Both the withdrawer and the pursuer will need to risk being vulnerable and letting go of their old ways of protecting one's heart and getting needs met. This means that daily, in every interaction with your spouse, you'll be conscious that you are building a healthier marriage and fostering a safe haven.

THE WITHDRAWER EMERGES AND CONNECTS

Keith has recently quit his job and started his own company. It is a big change for him and his wife, Annette, and it has come on the heels of their twin sons starting their senior year in high school. These changes have placed new demands on Keith and Annette's relationship. It places pressure on vulnerable areas, bringing to the surface some hurts that have been lurking in the shadows for many years.

"I don't think things will ever change between us," Annette told Keith one Saturday morning. "I've begged you to be more sensitive, to talk to me, pray with me, and be more romantic in ways that matter to me. But no matter how much I plead with you, we never seem to be on the same page."

Keith felt hurt by Annette's words. In fact, lately he has been feeling hurt by many of the things she's said. He feels hopeless—like she seldom appreciates his efforts and won't give him the space to take on hobbies. When he does try, she always seems to be disappointed in him. This particular morning, he dealt with his hurt as he always does. He shut down on the inside but kept smiling and going through the motions of the morning.

Several times during the day Annette asked Keith, "Is everything okay? Are you mad? Are we still okay?"

Each time Keith would answer, "Fine, dear. Nothing is wrong."

But it wasn't. Keith had reached a point where he was ready for change. And he knew that in order to bring about true change in his marriage, he would have to take a good, long look at himself and his own way of relating in the marriage. Doing so took him on a difficult and painful journey that had incredible rewards on the other side. Let's share his journey. And then we'll review Annette's journey of growth as the pursuer.

Becoming Aware of Your Cycle and the Feelings Under It

When Keith and Annette came into a counseling session the following week, he spoke up. "I'm becoming more and more aware of the feelings I have when Annette and I fight. Just like the other day, when she said that I didn't do anything to help her when she was pregnant. I was really hurt. She got angry and vented, and I reacted to her hostility by defending myself. She makes hurtful statements to me and I try to discount what she says. What she says might have validity, but the way she says it is hurtful. So, knowing that I can't change her mind, I shrink back from her anger. I just clam up and keep quiet."

Annette's eyes flashed while Keith was talking, but he continued, "When I feel she is attacking me, I close the doors to the different rooms in my heart. I slam them shut. I don't let her go near those doors. I direct her to another room that doesn't hurt so much when she is in it. In that room she can criticize me and it doesn't really matter."

Keith continued, "But I am tired of withdrawing and feeling unworthy and incompetent. I don't want to feel that way anymore. I don't want to withdraw anymore. I want to be able to share what I am feeling and have my wife accept me for who I am."

Ready for Change

Like Keith, spouses who withdraw often come to a point where they become dissatisfied with shrinking away from their partner's critical position. They no longer like the feeling of walking on eggshells around their spouse's moods. They grow weary of holding their breath, anticipating a fight, constantly being in the doghouse, and feeling unvalued by the person they love the most. Instead, they long to be able to speak up, to share openly and honestly. Sound risky? Yes, it is, especially for a spouse who has spent most of his or her married life dodging tough emotions and withdrawing from conflict.

Realizing the Risk of Coming Close

Most withdrawers would say that opening their heart and sharing their experiences with their spouse feels unsafe. They've learned that when they try to share their hearts with their spouse, it is not received, and now they are frustrated and don't know what more they can do. "Even when I share my deepest feelings," says Keith, "it's not good enough for Annette. I do my best and I disappoint her. So I've just pretty much stopped trying."

Of course, when Keith withdraws, Annette pursues him. He reports that he gets anxious feelings whenever she comes after him. And he admits that he pulls back in an attempt to deal with those feelings. Here's what he says about her pursuing mode: "It has hurt me very deeply to hear you criticize me and put me down. You make me feel like a dummy—unloved and unwanted and always in the doghouse. I wonder if I am as bad as you say I am. Maybe I'm a hypocrite or not good enough. I do struggle with some of the things you accuse me of. Maybe I'm as worthless as you say I am!"

Becoming Emotionally Engaged

It became evident as Keith began to share his fears of being hurt that he no longer wants to be withdrawn and actually yearns and desires to be connected. When withdrawers realize their hurts under their withdrawing, new feelings arise as to their position in the relationship. They no longer want to hide in the corner, shut down, or block out their spouse when they feel their spouse's emotional storm and criticism approaching. At this point, the withdrawing partner begins to take a new position in the relationship. Seeing themselves as valuable and desiring respect and appreciation, they slowly emotionally reengage. At first they may feel angry at their spouse or at themselves for being in a withdrawn position. Then their longing to be accepted and close draws them toward their spouse.

Instead of withdrawing as he has done for so long, Keith tried to share his needs. "Annette, I want to feel special to you. I want you to hold off on the criticism and not tell me how bad I am. I don't want to feel insignificant in this relationship anymore."

As Keith says this to his wife, he is engaged with his own emotional experience and speaks from an accessible rather than a distant and emotionally unavailable position. He says whatever he needs to say in order to open up his heart and express himself to his wife.

It's important to notice that Keith is not demanding that Annette change. He's the one who is changing, and this new way of expressing himself amounts to a major change for Keith. Many withdrawers, like Keith, have spent a chunk of their lives tiptoeing around their loved one. But now, instead of taking the backseat, they move to the front seat and engage their partner. They reconnect with the relationship, expressing their hurts in a nondefensive manner, sharing their longings openly and honestly, and describing what they need in order to come close.

Sharing Longings and Fears of Closeness

Too often, spouses ignore their longings for acceptance and intimacy for years, even decades. But when they finally acknowledge their feelings and understand what causes them to defend themselves and pull back, they quickly realize they don't want to hide anymore. They long to share their dreams, their thoughts, their feelings, and their ideas with their spouse. They begin to see themselves differently, as a participant in the relationship, and they ask their spouse to do the same. Here's what Keith said:

> I long to open the other doors of my heart and have you enter the other rooms. I long to let you see the different parts of me. And I

hope you'll accept those parts of me and be comfortable with me. I want you to value me, all of me. I also want to take care of you, Annette. I want to be the man you respect most in the world. I want you to let me love you. I want to feel that you value me and enjoy me. I guess what I'm really saying is . . . I want to be accepted by you, just the way I am.

Trusting Change: Overcoming Doubt and Disbelief

Although each spouse has longed for change, when it starts to happen, it is difficult to believe that it is genuine and will continue. For many spouses, change comes only after months, if not years, of hurts. These hurts often go back to the very beginning of the marriage.

Keith had come from a family where emotions were not shared. Instead, they were numbed and neutralized. Both he and Annette were young when they married and didn't know how to make sense of their own emotions, never mind each other's. So when Annette expressed herself, Keith would shut her down. He told her to "get over it" or to go talk to her mother. He regrets having acted so harshly, because it deeply hurt Annette and he has paid for it ever since. Annette fears that Keith will not consider her perspective or make decisions that are in the best interest of the relationship. She has come to believe that Keith shuts her out because he is self-centered and doesn't want to be close.

Keith admits, "Many a time, I wasn't there when Annette needed me. I withdrew and discounted her feelings. I understand why she had to come after me. But I want to do it differently now, and I need her to help me understand how to connect with her in a way that works for both of us."

"I want the same thing," Annette tells him, "but to be honest, I can't quite believe this is going to work. It's going to take me a while to be sure." Like many other spouses in her position, Annette is afraid that the change is only temporary. It's hard for her to trust it, and that's understandable.

I (Sharon) reminded them both, "You can't, after one week, or even one month, give up and say, 'Hey, we tried this for a month and it didn't work, so there's no use going on with it. We'll just go back to our old ways.'

Remember, change isn't just about getting something from each other. You change because you want to grow and mature as a person. God calls you to be the best person you can be, and that's true no matter what happens between you, even when you have setbacks."

And there will be setbacks.

Persevering Through Setbacks

The minute you see your spouse roll his eyes, the instant you feel her steel walls going up, you may become overwhelmed with frustration and anger. That's what happened when Annette heard Keith say, "You're acting just like your mother when you try to twist my arm like that!" To her it implied that she was controlling, manipulative, and didn't allow him any space to be himself. This made her feel really bad about herself.

Annette admits, "I fight against feeling controlling, which is exactly the way my mother was. I know I can be like that, and when he says I am, it feels like he is rejecting me. So I fight back by telling him how wrong he is and how okay I am."

Annette learned that when she fights back, she is sending Keith the message that it is unsafe to be vulnerable with her. She began to accept the fact that even though she longs for Keith to come close and share himself with her, her negative reactions have a powerful impact on him, causing him to close his heart and spirit toward her.

THE PURSUER SOFTENS AND CONNECTS

We've taken a close look at Keith, the withdrawer. Now what about the experience of Annette, the pursuer, as she grows to be more vulnerable and close?

For as long as she can remember, Annette has tried to either crawl under Keith's shell or crack it open. Those seemed to be the only ways she could draw close to his heart, but they never worked. This was not only frustrating for her, but also very painful. Now, as she senses Keith's desire to become more engaged, she begins to soften and risks being vulnerable instead of always nagging, being angry, or panicking when she senses a disconnection.

As Annette reflects on her emotional responses, she becomes more open to new ways of understanding herself and Keith. This begins to remove the necessity for the pursue-withdraw cycle. Instead, a new cycle begins, one where Keith is emotionally connected and can be found by Annette, and where Annette no longer needs to pursue and fight to get Keith's attention. At last they are able to be more emotionally available to one another. Let's walk with Annette through her experience of emotionally connecting.

Understanding Why the Pursuit Happens

Let's let Annette share her perspective of the hurts and frustrations in her marriage. She has often felt alone and on her own when Keith has withdrawn into his independent world. She recalls some specific times when he has left her alone: when the twins were born, when she went back to school, and when he joined the bowling league.

Annette says, "Keith has always cut off my ideas and thoughts; he doesn't listen to any other view except his own. He is not patient with my feelings. I have to talk things over before I make a decision, and he just comes to a fast conclusion and the subject is closed. He shuts me out. And yes, I push him. Why? Because I want him to give me a reaction. His silence makes me feel rejected and unloved. To be honest, those are terrifying feelings."

Annette has come to understand her emotional experience when she is hurt. She realizes that her blood begins to boil, her emotions start to heat up, and her words become harsh and critical. "I know I have made good points, and I might even have been right, but in powering through my side of the story, I somehow hurt Keith and pushed him away. I don't mean to, but I don't know any other way to reach him."

In order to get her husband's attention, Annette has tried controlling, reacting, pursuing, nagging, and exploding. Yet she feels she never is able to really connect with him, that he is always one step away from her reach. "I fight for him to see my view, to see my hurt. Yet he goes right on defending himself, telling me I am wrong to feel the way I do and finally shutting me out again. He does what he is doing even though he knows I don't want him to. It's like he is saying to me, 'What you want doesn't matter to me!' How am I supposed to believe he really cares?"

Searching for Soft Feelings

Now, however, rather than focusing on Keith's faults, Annette focuses on her own inner experience. She stays with her softer feelings instead of clicking into anger or blame and begins to realize that under her anger and hurt she feels abandoned. Even now, she is not so quick to reach for Keith and share her feelings with him. She has come to believe that needing him is a bad feeling, evidence that she is "weak." Annette remembers the relationship rule she has come to live by: "I promised to never count on anyone again. You can't be vulnerable; you'll be betrayed."

Asking for Understanding

But because Keith is now willing to be more emotionally connected with Annette, she is willing to risk vulnerability. Like other pursuers, at this point Annette expresses her need to feel safe with Keith and her need for him to listen and hold her perspective. Annette's needs now come forward and she explains, "I want you to hold me, to help me feel safe." She quietly expresses her attachment needs. Without demanding, negotiating, or blaming, she asks for her needs to be met.

Speaking Words of Kindness

From a place of honesty, openness, and gentleness, she reaches for Keith and risks to ask him to come close. "You are irreplaceable," she tells him, "and I need you in my life. I want to be close to you, not just to have you provide for the family. I need you to be there for me, to hold me when I feel alone or feel like everything's going wrong. I long for you to know me and love all of me."

This time, Annette is able to present her requests in a manner that pulls Keith in, increasing the possibility that he will respond. The more Keith is able to be emotionally engaged, the more Annette is able to lean on him and trust that he finds her valuable and worthy. At this point husbands like Keith are surprised to discover that underneath all the porcupine quills is a tender wife who values them deeply and longs to be close, loved, and understood.

Accepting Change: Moving Beyond Doubts

But again the question arises, Will this last? If you are usually the one who withdraws, and you see these changes in your pursuing spouse, you may walk gingerly for a while, waiting for the other shoe to drop. *When will he start criticizing again? When will she blow up and let me have it? When will the peace be shattered by another explosion?* Accepting change is difficult. And we are bound to ask, "How can I be sure you won't go back to your old way of responding?" Only time and repeated positive experiences with your spouse will give you assurance.

And as you both grow into new roles and responses, humble yourselves, and ask for help from each other: "I need for you to teach me. Maybe we can figure this out together. I really do want to know how to come close to you. Please help me."

Why Don't You Know? Don't You Love Me?

This brings us to a common pitfall. For some reason, couples often come into marriage thinking that their husband or wife should know exactly what they need. They have the idea that if they have to show or tell their spouse what to do to be more loving or caring, it indicates that the spouse doesn't love them. This is simply not true. To the contrary, husbands and wives need to develop an open communication system where they are able to share their needs and longings.

We have to teach each other what feels good; we have to let our spouse know how to nurture us in a special way that feels just right. Do you dream of love notes and words of tenderness? Do you long for touch and caresses? Does love, for you, mean kind deeds and a helping hand? Do you crave playful companionship? Surprises? Special gifts? Talk about it. Make it clear. Teach your spouse what will make you feel loved and cared for. And when your spouse tells you his needs, make sure you respond promptly and wholeheartedly!

You'll also need to communicate ways to restore your emotional connection after a hurtful incident. Each couple has a language of their own. A wife may cup her husband's face in her hands, hold his cheeks in the warmth of her palms, gaze into his eyes, and say, "I cherish you sweetheart, and I am sorry for what happened."

A husband may offer a gentle neck rub, or offer to help with the dishes. Or he may extend on overture for sex. And this is an important point: For a man, sex is a way to reconnect with his wife through touching, caressing, and unconditional acceptance. It is not just a release of built-up energy or the selfish satisfaction of a physical need. Sex is a powerful means of connection for a man, and for some women. His or her spouse needs to respect that. It may well be very different from the way *you* might choose to connect, but it is very real and necessary and important. On the other hand, withholding sex is too often a way of saying, "I'm still in control. I am not quite ready to give myself to you fully or completely." Discovering together the ways to reconnect after an argument will help dissolve resentment and shorten the postfight disconnection.

Putting It All Together

Perhaps by now, you have walked through the process of turning your emotionally disconnected relationship into a safe haven marriage. This has not, of course, been an easy process, and has required each of you to become vulnerable and to risk putting your hearts into each other's hands. But the blessings that have followed have been bountiful. You now are beginning to experience each other as a safe place where you know you are loved, seen, and accepted. You and your spouse can count on one another to be trustworthy, emotionally available, and responsive. Your marriage has become, or is on the path to becoming, a safe haven.

But perhaps, as you reach out to grow and to be more vulnerable with your spouse, something tugs at your heart, reminding you to be cautious, not to take risks or become too vulnerable. Each time you feel yourself moving closer to your spouse, something triggers an argument or opens an old wound.

As we said at the beginning of the book, some men and women are so injured by childhood abuse or trauma that they simply cannot bring themselves to open up. If this is the case with you or your spouse, please find a godly counselor who is willing to help you work through this process as a couple or, if necessary, individually. Do the same if you are finding it impossible to identify and express your feelings. Also, if your spouse is unwilling to open up or to work through the reattachment process with you, please find help for yourself.

But perhaps it's something else. Maybe you are still struggling with a hurt that is so deep and painful that it seems as if it will never heal. It may be something that keeps you just one step from risking enough to find your way into your safe haven. This old hurt that has not healed may be what counselors call an attachment injury. In the next chapter, we will share how to heal your heart from such hurts that keep you and your spouse from risking to truly love again.

REFLECTION QUESTIONS

1. Of the ways of understanding how you argue, which ones are hardest for you? In which areas are you strongest?

   - Resisting battling over who said what when
   - Pulling back in a fight and talking about how you are fighting
   - Moving toward understanding and acceptance of each other
   - Respecting each other's feelings and perspective in the heat of the fight
   - Using clarification communication to gain understanding before reacting
   - Being willing to be influenced by your spouse and to do things differently

2. Read through the process of emotionally engaging for the withdrawer and the pursuer. How would you like to grow beyond being a withdrawer or a pursuer?

3. In an attempt to accept and move closer to your spouse, what is your spouse's experience as a withdrawer or a pursuer? Try to make sense of how and why your spouse responds the way he or she does in the relationship.

4. What makes you feel seen, understood, and loved by your spouse? What helps you and your spouse reconnect after an argument? Is it touch, words, space, kind deeds, a helping hand?

Chapter 9

HEALING HURTS OF THE HEART

> *My dove in the clefts of the rock, in the hiding places on the moun-*
> *tainside, show me your face, let me hear your voice; for your voice is*
> *sweet. . . . Catch for us the foxes, the little foxes that ruin . . . our vine-*
> *yards that are in bloom.*
>
> —SONG OF SONGS 2:14–15

Some hurts just don't go away. In some marriages, they keep resurfacing over and over again, like scum in a dirty pond. The "wounding event" gets thrown into every quarrel and gets rehearsed and reviewed at every squabble, stirring up fresh anger, tears, and frustration. And no matter what the offending spouse tries to do, the wound he or she inflicted sometime in the past just won't go away. How many times must a couple talk about an injurious event? How much must a guilty partner apologize before the problem is resolved?

These healing-resistant, wounding events become like land mines. They stay hidden inside innocent comments, quiet evening outings, or small mishaps, waiting for just one misstep. When touched, they explode. In this way they become recurring themes that can bruise the relationship of even the best-intentioned couples.

The wounded and the wounder experience these resistant injuries differently. For wounded spouses, life may go along fine for a while. Then suddenly some minor incident reminds them of that terrible time when they were left out in the cold—forgotten, demeaned, betrayed, or deeply offended. And these wounds just don't dissolve with a spur-of-the-moment "I *said* I was sorry" by the wounding spouse.

When the wounded husband or wife hears, "I *said* I was sorry," he or she strikes back with a counterattack of criticism, blame, accusations, and anger. The need to be understood is so compelling that it controls the wounded spouse's words, and the only actions that seem possible are those that hurt back.

Meanwhile, for the spouse who caused the wound, the constant reviewing of the event only serves to build up more defensiveness. No matter how much he or she asks for forgiveness, the spouse just can't, or won't, let it go. So the wounder has become sick and tired of hearing their spouse moan and complain about what happened and becomes angry and defensive every time the subject is brought up. Or the wounder avoids all topics that could possibly lead to discussing the offending event. "Are you bringing this up again? I don't want to talk about it. I said I am sorry and don't know what else I can do. It's not that big of a deal. It was just a bump in the road, so let it go!"

For the wounded spouse, a response that cuts off all recollection of the hurt is a "double injury." The denial adds insult to injury. They are left holding the hurt in their hands, not knowing where to put it. They are cut off from trying to make sense of what happened, and this leaves them even more confused about their own reaction than their partner is about his behavior. In such a standoff, the couple remains emotionally disconnected, and the bond between them is no longer safe. Neither partner is a source of comfort or security to the other.

Unresolved hurts like this, which build up a wall between spouses, are called "attachment wounds." Such attachment wounds change the way partners view one another, their relationship, and their future together, which is why such injuries need to be dealt with quickly and decisively. Otherwise, each spouse comes to see the other as emotionally unsafe.

A CLOSER LOOK AT ATTACHMENT WOUNDS

What makes some wounds resistant to healing, while others seem to resolve themselves without much trouble? To answer this question we need to take a closer look at the nature of the emotional bond that forms in marriage, or in any other meaningful relationship.

The Importance of Your Attachment Bond

The strong connection that forms between you and your spouse is an attachment bond, and this must be present before it can be wounded. Strangers don't cause attachment wounds because there is no bond to threaten.

An attachment bond is an emotional connection you make to a specific, irreplaceable person. Deep within our hearts God created us for such bonds. It is what drives us to seek close relationships. We all need the warmth and security of a close relationship in order to grow and become healthy men and women. It is in our close relationships that we discover who we are. Through them we experience our own lovability and worthiness, and, just as important, we discover how others can or can't be emotionally safe.

If you are married, marriage becomes your most treasured relationship. To our marriages we bring our hopes and longings to be loved. We cherish growing old together. In the shelter of each other, we live life and become all God has for both of us to become. If our spouse is emotionally available and accessible to us, he responds to our needs in sensitive ways. In our spouse, we find acceptance, love, and support. As our marriage matures, the emotional attachment bond between our spouse and us becomes close, safe, trustworthy, and predictable, and our marriage becomes our safe haven.

The Violation of Basic Expectations

In marriage we rightly expect our partner to be attentive, responsive, and supportive, at least most of the time, and we hope that our spouse will be there when we reach out. We anticipate a husband's touch when we are hurt, a wife's smile when we need encouragement, and a warm, familiar presence when we need support.

But suppose this doesn't happen. What then? Attachment injuries disrupt the precious bond that connects you and your spouse. The bond is bruised and becomes fragile; the relationship, once strong, now feels shaky. An attachment injury leaves you feeling abandoned and forsaken. "You left me; I was so alone; it was like you threw me aside and didn't consider me at all," was how one wife described it. The deep assurance that no matter what happens between the two of you, your spouse will always be there for you is shattered. A host of doubts and a deep sense of insecurity arise. You begin to reevaluate your sense of self-worth: "I was just not important enough to her." "I wasn't valued. I just didn't matter to him."

EVENTS THAT WOUND

The actual event that triggers an attachment injury doesn't necessarily occur in isolation. Often a couple is already experiencing a threadbare connection with each other for any number of reasons. One specific incident, however, becomes a "symbolic marker" of the relationship's insecure bond.

What kinds of incidents become attachment injuries? Attachment injuries usually occur around the birth of a child, during times of illness, during life transitions (new job, kids start school, leave home), or during a loss (death of relative, job loss).[1] The injury can occur as a result of disappointment over some vitally important event, such as your husband's going back to work the day after your second baby was born, when you desperately needed his help, or over some small event as when your wife refused to bring your dinner to you in the den when you wanted to catch the final minutes of a football game on television. As we'll see later in the chapter, it can also be a major betrayal caused by pornography or an extramarital affair. But an attachment injury can begin in seemingly small ways, such as:

- You begin to cry. Your husband laughs at you and sarcastically says, "Is the big baby going to cry now?" Something inside you is deeply hurt, and your husband suddenly seems unsafe, uncaring, and not to be trusted with your emotions.
- Your wife had an "inappropriate friendship" fifteen years ago. You have forgiven her, but your heart just can't seem to fully reconnect.
- You really needed your husband's support when you went in for a scary

medical test, and he chose to go to the office instead. You felt abandoned, facing the fear and pain all alone.

- Your husband failed to call you while he was away on a business trip. You're still questioning his whereabouts that night, and you haven't quite trusted him since.

- You got home from a weekend business trip and your husband hadn't done the dishes, bathed the children, or fed the dog. He was watching television and barely said hello when you walked in the door. You realized no one would take care of you or be there for you.

- You shared with your wife your struggles with pornography, and she got angry and brushed you off, saying, "You are so sick!" You conclude that she will never understand that part of you and it would have been better to have kept it a secret.

- You got back from the hospital after surgery, and your husband didn't come into the bedroom all day to ask how you were doing. You felt abandoned, alone, left to take care of yourself.

- Your wife criticized you and embarrassed you in front of your colleagues at a company dinner. You felt rejected and humiliated by her and promised yourself never to include her in your inner life.

- Your husband threatened to divorce you in the middle of a fight. You realize that nothing is certain, even the love of your spouse.

- Your wife angrily says that the two of you should never have married. You've always feared that she would someday leave you, and now you suspect that at any time you may be left alone.

- Your husband fails to defend you in a conversation with your in-laws. You feel alone, misunderstood, and conclude that he will never come to your side when you need him.

HOW ATTACHMENT BOND INJURIES HAPPEN

Not all hurts and disappointments become attachment wounds, and the bond is not harmed every time a spouse is unavailable or unresponsive. Many times couples are late to one another's appointments, don't show up to family events, say the wrong things, are insensitive, or forget to do what they promised. These hurts are somehow just folded into the larger scope of the relationship. In these instances, the husband or wife is still seen as valuable, and the hurt can still be discussed and healed.

Offenses become damaging when a spouse is vulnerable, when comfort from their partner is essential, when the vulnerable partner is in special need of support, and it's not there. Let's explore why certain events wound the heart in such a way that forgiveness and emotional reconnection seem next to impossible.

The Devastating Experience of Feeling Abandoned

Spouses who have experienced attachment injuries talk about the sense of being abandoned and left to care for themselves in life-and-death terms: "You left me to die inside." "I was so overwhelmed and alone, and you let me down." "When you didn't show up, something inside me just died." "When you said that, I promised myself I would never open and share my heart with you again."

Failed Attempts to Bring About Healing

The relationship is then organized around the injured partner, with the other spouse trying to get the injured partner to be emotionally available and responsive again. But it doesn't work. Instead, the spouse who caused the hurt is self-protective, defensive, and continues to withdraw from the seemingly irresolvable confrontation. The hurt stays alive, uncomforted, and unhealed.

The injured spouse longs to come close to the wounder, to be seen, understood, and to have the bond healed. But the wounder's inability to understand the injury results in failed attempts at reconnection, and the couple remains emotionally apart. The injured spouse swings between trying to come close and then pushing away in hurt. Later he may swing to the other extreme of numbing and withdrawing.

Failed attempts to restore the bond continue to confirm that the offending partner is unpredictable and unsafe. The hurt partner cannot or will not let go of the injury no matter how much the other apologizes. Thus the unresolved hurt becomes the topic of constant bickering. It may even lie dormant for a while, but will eventually reemerge with a vengeance when some small incident triggers the pain.

Here are the kinds of things you'll hear couples saying when they have an attachment injury:

"My hurt didn't matter to you."

"When I needed you most, you shut me out."

"You are irrational about what happened."

"You can't even understand how that hurt me."

"If you can shut me out when I need you the most, then why would I ever trust you with my heart? I'm never going to put myself in your hands again!"

ATTEMPTS TO REPAIR: WHEN MORE OF THE SAME DOESN'T WORK

Couples unsuccessfully try to heal their hurts by repeatedly reviewing the incident, blaming each other, and defending themselves. Let's take a look at how couples typically deal with attachment hurts. Perhaps this will help you to better understand your own circumstances, show you why your attempts have failed, and guide you toward a better way.

The Hurt Is Repeatedly Brought Up by the Injured Spouse

Harry and Brittany always circled round and round the event that wounded Brittany, never really arriving at any resolve or healing. She usually says something like, "You were so insensitive to me. Just like the time I was going to take my big test, and the day before you wanted to go out with your friends. You left me alone to take care of the kids and to try to study at the same time. I felt so alone. No wonder I failed! You abandoned me. I always have to take care of myself!"

The Person Who Did the Hurting Defends Him- or Herself

Typically, the spouse who is accused of inflicting the injury responds by taking a defensive position. Harry says, "Not again! You're bringing this up again? I can't believe you."

He discounts the hurt. "You know, it wasn't that bad. It's just that you overreacted." Then he denies the impact. "I don't know why you took it that way and made it into something far worse than it was."

Harry minimized the incident and Brittany's pain. "It really wasn't that big of a deal. You already had a feeling that you'd failed your test, so why was it such a big deal once you got your failing grade? You can take it over again. You are making a mountain out of a molehill!"

These comments are defensive, intended to shift the blame. It is understandable that Harry would do that: Who would want to be painted as the hurtful spouse who wounded his partner? But the deflecting of blame hinders acknowledgment and understanding of the pain, leaving the wounded spouse unable to heal.

Injury Is Confirmed . . . Again

Every time Joan tries to repair the hurt and to elicit a caring response from Russell, she is wounded all over again by his defensiveness. She tries to talk to Russell about how she felt the night of her miscarriage. "You have no idea how alone I felt that night—all alone with such a terrible heartbreak."

Months later, she still brings it up as proof that Russell is not there for her and that she has to take care of herself. Russell never knows what to say to make it okay for her, so he defends himself, minimizes the event, and discounts her hurt. And again she experiences him as emotionally unavailable and insensitive. This confirms to her that he doesn't care about her feelings. He hasn't been sensitive in the past, isn't now, and probably won't be in the future.

MOVING BEYOND FORGIVENESS

Healing attachment wounds requires both partners to be good forgivers. But while the giving and receiving of forgiveness is of vital importance, it is not enough. Forgiveness is a necessary first step toward mending attachment injuries, but it does not necessarily lead to reconnection of the attachment bond. For the well-being of your heart as well as your marriage, you'll need to give up your right to hurt your spouse in return. You forgive the wrong that was done to you, because you recognize the grace and mercy that Jesus has freely offered to you. He has asked you, in response, to forgive those who hurt and wound you.

When spousal trust has been betrayed, it takes time and effort to heal the wounds. Trust has to be rebuilt, and the injured spouse will have to learn through repeated experiences that you are again someone in whom she can trust. You have to be patient and allow your partner to learn how to rebuild this trust.

The steps toward forgiveness are found elsewhere, and we recommend you gain an understanding of forgiveness if you have an attachment injury. But to reconnect emotionally and to see your spouse once again as reliable, safe, and a source of comfort requires additional, intentional restorative work. The steps toward healing your attachment bond and reconnecting your hearts are outlined here.

Reconnecting is a risky business. It means that both you and your spouse will have to become vulnerable again. You will, once more, need to live out the tender Afrikaans expressions I learned growing up: "*Ek het jou lief*" (I have your heart), and "*Ek vou jou my lief terig gee*" (I want to give you my heart back).

The fact is, you haven't succeeded before at healing your marital wounds. So we offer the following steps as a different and healthier way to approach your spouse about injuries to your attachment bond. We recommend finding a quiet place, free of distractions, to think about the following steps together. And remember, this is not a one-time-and-you-are-done process. You may have to review aspects of these steps many times over in order to bring about healing. And if this process seems to reopen the wound and trigger more fighting, then we recommend walking through it with a coun-selor or pastor.

Here's how one couple worked through the process. Meet Larry and Michelle.

Michelle: "My mother died in a car accident. I came home from the hospital to find that you had gone to Home Depot to buy *sprinklers*. I couldn't believe it! How could you do that if you cared about me?"

Larry: "Yes, I *did* care about you. I *do* care about you. We keep going over this. I worked hard installing the sprinklers in the yard that weekend, just for you."

Michelle: "Then you left for the desert to go play golf."

Larry: "Sorry, but your sisters came into town and you were going through your mother's stuff with them. You didn't need me there."

Michelle: "My mother died, and then you left me to die inside. You just don't get it. You just weren't there for me."

Larry: "I'm sorry. How many times do I have to say I am sorry? You refuse to let it go. No matter what I do or say, it always comes up."

Here's another couple's story. Meet Max and Erica.

Erica didn't want anything to happen, it was just fun at first and seemed innocent enough. So what if she stopped for coffee after work with Tony? It was exciting to have a man find her so attractive and enjoyable. She had no intention of it getting out of hand. After all, she had just met him five months ago at the office, and besides, she was married.

It wasn't long before Erica found herself dressing to please Tony and making excuses for coming home late so she could go with Tony for coffee after work. Arriving home extra late one day, she had difficulty coming up with an excuse. She realized, *What am I doing? I love my husband. Even though things are rocky right now, I don't want to be involved with anyone else but Max.*

The following Saturday she couldn't keep the secret any longer and finally told her husband what she had been doing the past several weeks. He listened. They cried. He took time to think about it. He knew he didn't want to leave her. He was very hurt but he could forgive her. Still, his pain went deeper into his heart. How could the woman he loved do this? How could he risk trusting her again? He forgave her, but could he emotionally reconnect and give her his heart again?

STEPS TOWARD HEALING AND RESTORATION OF THE ATTACHMENT BOND

Here are the steps these couples learned to take in order to restore their attachment bond and heal their hurts.

Step One: Share Your Hurt

The spouse who is wounded needs to share how his heart has been hurt. Explain how the injury has harmed your attachment bond. Tell your story. Describe the incident in which you felt abandoned, hurt, or wounded. From your heart, how did this incident hurt you? Why was this event significant?

Don't criticize your partner's character or highlight her faults. It is very tempting to do so because you feel so justified in your hurt and anger. But this is not the way of forgiveness. Instead, describe the feelings that lie beneath your anger, frustration, and resentfulness. Explain how the incident has injured you. Maybe you felt sadness, helplessness, fear, shame, abandonment, and rejection—whatever words you use, let your spouse know that it is because of your deep love for her that your hurt is so painful.

Maybe you shared defenseless, raw emotions with your spouse right after the incident. But at that time, he was unable to respond in a way that made you feel seen or understood, so your heart could not trust again. Over time you placed a hard "candy" coating around those tender feelings and became angry, critical, resentful, and disrespectful. You wanted to make sure your spouse was not going to ignore your pain.

Or, if you were too wounded to deal with the pain, perhaps you felt that the best response was no response, and so you withdrew. Explain how you have attempted to deal with your pain and how it might possibly have damaged your relationship.

Here are some ways others have described their feelings:

- "I feel so afraid and hurt. I criticize and attack so you can't ignore me. I won't let you refuse to look at my pain. I thought the one person I could turn to when I was so hurt would be you, and you weren't there."
- "I felt abandoned, like there was no one in the world for me. I didn't know where to turn. I didn't want to be comforted by other people. I wanted you to comfort me. I was sad and lonely."
- "I was so hurt after you had that fling with your friend at work that I shut down on the inside. I pulled back. I processed it on my own."
- "I always thought we would be true to each other, no matter how bad

things got. I feel worthless, like I have failed as a husband. I feel alone and broken inside."

Step Two: Understand the Significance of the Hurt

The wounder needs to understand the significance of the event to his partner. Do you remember the old Indian proverb that says if you really want to understand someone you should walk a mile in his moccasins? This principle can go a long way toward healing your relationship. With your imagination in one hand and your heart in the other, try to put yourself in your spouse's position.

You need to try to make sense of why your spouse reacted the way she did. You may not agree with your spouse's feelings or response, but this is your spouse's attachment injury, not yours. You might react differently if it happened to you, or you might not. It doesn't matter. Your spouse's energy, all these months and years, was probably focused on yelling, blaming, criticizing, or shutting down. But rather than just seeing this behavior on the surface, try putting yourself in your spouse's shoes for a while. Why the reaction? Is it merely that she is hysterical and cannot make any sense whatsoever, or is it that she really was deeply hurt? Is he overly sensitive, too emotional with no control of his reactions? Probably not, if you'll just take the trouble to understand.

As you listen to what this incident meant to your spouse, you will gain a deeper understanding of your spouse's heart. You will also understand the significance of the event. You'll begin to realize that all this has happened because of your importance to your spouse, not because of your inadequacies or insensitivity. For now, separate your self-esteem and pride from your spouse's reaction. Sometimes saying nothing in response is the best thing. Just be sure to let your spouse know that you are listening, and listening very carefully.

Step Three: Express Your Emotions

The spouse who is wounded needs to express his tender emotions and grief from a place of vulnerability. And the spouse who did the wounding needs to acknowledge his or her partner's pain and hurt.

Listen to your partner's pain without defending yourself. This might be very difficult to do. You may not agree with how your spouse interprets the event, but realize that she is entitled to her feelings, interpretation, and experience. For certain reasons, the incident was an attachment wound for your spouse.

Step Four: Share How the Event Evolved

The wounder needs to share how the event evolved. Describe what you did and why you did it. Explain your view so your spouse can see your heart, your intentions, and why it made sense for you to do what you did. In this way you shift from being an unpredictable and unknown person to being predictable, with your actions making sense. Your spouse won't feel so vulnerable if you help him understand that he will not be suddenly, out of the blue, hurt again.

As you share, don't be defensive or try to minimize the incident. Don't twist the truth. That will just catapult you back into your marital cycle of blame and defense, which will only injure you both.

Let's look in on Larry and Michelle again. Larry says, "I froze when I heard your mother had died. I wanted to cry, but I thought if I did, I'd never stop. I didn't know what to do. So I got busy digging the ditches for the sprinkler system. You had always complained that we didn't have sprinklers in the front yard, and I wanted to please you."

Remember Erica's infatuation and Eric's hurt. Listen to what Erica says to Max: "I was always Daddy's little girl who got all the attention. Somehow it fed my self-esteem when Tony was attracted to me. I feel embarrassed to say this, but it also feels good to finally be really honest with you. I so wanted your attention, but we always seemed too busy, and we were always fighting during that time."

Step Five: Understand the Wounder's Perspective

The spouse who was wounded needs to try to understand the wounder's point of view. As you make sense of why your spouse thought and did what he did, you will be able to hold your spouse's perspective in one hand, and your own perspective in the other. This will require courage. You fear that if you listen, and gain understanding or compassion, you won't be entitled to your own pain and perspective. Worse, you may be afraid that you'll somehow be condoning something very wrong. But that's not the case. As you hold your spouse's experience alongside your own, your spouse is able to do the same for you. Out of your vulnerability, not out of your anger, share your heart, rather than blame or be defensive, insisting, "Never again will I trust you!"

Michelle says to Larry, "I think I understand. You tried to comfort me by putting in sprinklers and giving me space with my sisters. You were giving me the best you had at that time. You actually were very sad over my mom's death too. So much so that you didn't know what to do with your pain. I am so sorry; I didn't know."

In a similar way, Max turns to Erica. "I may never fully understand why you made the choice to start up a relationship with Tony," he says, "and I'll always be hurt by what you did. It was very wrong. But I understand that you were lonely and tried to get my attention. You longed for friendship and to be seen, and I know we weren't getting along all that well."

Step Six: Take Responsibility

The wounder needs to take responsibility for her part in the problem. As you stay emotionally engaged and listen to your spouse's hurts, you come to realize and take responsibility for your contribution to the injury. You may need to express how much you regret having done what you did. You may want to share your remorse, and show compassion for the hurt you and your spouse have experienced. This may sound foreign or strange to you as you read this, but as you walk through the previous steps, this step will naturally follow.

Erica admits to Max, "The relationship I had with Tony was inappropriate. I should never have dealt with my pain and loneliness that way. It has been destructive. It has eaten away at me. It has devastated us both, and I would give anything to have dealt with our troubles differently. I am so sorry."

Larry says to Michelle, "Despite all my efforts to help you deal with your mom's death, I guess you were left to cry alone. I see how that has hurt you."

Step Seven: Ask for Comfort and Reassurance

The spouse who was wounded needs to ask for comfort and reassurance.

"I was so devastated when I found out that you were hanging out with Tony," Max explains to Erica. "I felt so alone. And the thought that you might leave me, that I might have to live without you, was terrible. I need to know you will never deal with your unhappiness with us that way again. You have to talk with me if you feel that unhappy in our relationship. And I want you to be able to bring your humanness into the marriage and to talk to me about it when you feel attracted to other men. I need to know you will first tell me before going off and having an affair. I need you to hold me. Understand that I am trying to heal, but I just need your reassurance."

Michelle asks of Larry, "I would like for you to hold me. Maybe we can go to my mother's grave together. I just need to know you see how this has hurt me."

Step Eight: Be Available to Your Spouse

The wounder needs, this time, to be there. The spouse who caused the injury is now able to respond in a caring manner. A new bonding experience can finally take place. In this emotionally corrective experience, the hurt husband is able to access his pain and reach for his wife, and this time the wife is available to him. It is this new experience that heals and redefines the relationship as safe again.

Larry: "Can I hold you, Michelle? I am so sorry your mom died. After my mother died, your mom was like my mom too. It is very sad. I'll be right here for you whenever you need support."

Erica: "I do value you, Max, and never want to hurt you this way again. I treasure the man you are. I long for us to be closer, to be better friends. I want to work on our relationship and put all my efforts with you."

WRITING A NEW STORY

Now both you and your spouse are able to rewrite a new story surrounding the event. This story includes a clear and acceptable view of how and why each of you responded. The questions "Why did you do that?" and "How could you have done that to me?" now have answers. Each spouse's pain and perspective are acknowledged and respected.

Husband and wife alike become predictable again. One doesn't feel like the unforgivable sinner. The other doesn't feel like an abandoned victim. Both are able to create a safe emotional connection. The relationship is redefined as a safe haven.

INJURIES OF THE DEEPEST KIND

Some injuries cut deeper than others and are so commonly found in marital therapy that we feel they should be singled out and highlighted here. Shocking as it is, more than half of all marriages will eventually struggle with one or both of these issues at one time or another. They are more devastating to the marital bond than most anything else. The two are both sex-related: pornography and extramarital affairs.

You can't downplay or dismiss the profound impact these behaviors have on the bond between a husband and wife. They inflict deep wounds. Why? Because they violate trust in the bond; they injure the tie that connects one spouse with the other. They not only break trust, but they revoke the emotional safety of the relationship.

Couples can weather many difficulties. They may disagree, argue, fight, defend, pursue, and not agree on anything. Yet still, deep down, each of them knows without a doubt that the bond that connects them is there, protected, safe, and certain. But when one partner takes sex outside the relationship, that bond is broken.

PLAYING WITH PORNOGRAPHY

It seemed innocent enough at first. *No one is getting hurt, and anyway, it's better than going out and having an affair,* Jim thought. Many an evening he would leave the bedroom, go downstairs to his office, and surf through the pornography sites on the Internet. They were easy to access; in fact, they seemed to find him—such is the skill of those who devise them. Even at the office he could close his door when things were not so busy and click away on the pornography sites whenever he felt the urge. At first it was just curiosity that drove him to it. Before long, it became exciting, even addictive. Eventually, it became a habit so powerful that Jim couldn't seem to break it.

Jim is drawn to pornography by a rush, a thrill, an irresistible sense of excitement. Once he feels it coming on, he is pulled in. Afterward, when the guilt becomes overwhelming, he promises himself that he won't do it again. He feels dirty, compromised, and ashamed. Then he wonders if he is being too hard on himself. *It's not such a big deal,* he tells himself, and life goes back to normal—until he feels the urge again. A strong addiction cycle pulls him in and keeps him in a loop that he can't stop on his own. Even getting caught in the act at work and accused of wasting his boss's time and money wasn't enough to scare him off. In fact, the more risky his habit became, the more exciting it was.

Jim began to wonder what it would be like if his wife, Kate, found out. Should he tell her? In many ways, he wanted to give up the pornography cycle, and he puzzled over what she would say if she knew. *She would hit the roof,* he warned himself. But maybe he needed her help in breaking this very powerful habit. Should he keep her out of it and try to deal with it on his own? Like most men, he took the course of least resistance and opted to say nothing. Weeks passed.

One night Kate awakened and realized Jim had left the bed. She began to wander around the house looking for him. She softly walked down the stairs, across the hallway, and to his office doorway. He heard her coming up behind him and quickly clicked the mouse to close the Web site. But she caught a glimpse of an obscene female image before it vanished.

He scolded her, "What are you doing sneaking up on me like that? Why are you spying on me?"

Kate was speechless. *Did I do something wrong?* she wondered. Then the images popped back up into her mind. *No!* "What do you mean what am I doing? What are *you* doing?" she demanded.

Jim angrily defended himself. "I have no idea what you're talking about! You're so paranoid. You've got nothing to worry about! Go back to bed!"

Her head spinning, Kate found her way back to bed, wondering what it all meant. But she couldn't sleep—the image she saw was burned into her memory. Something inside of her wouldn't allow her to let it go. The more she thought about it, the worse it became. Something in her heart broke. She felt betrayed, violated. The man she trusted with her whole heart, with her life and her dreams, had taken a sword to her heart. And she felt afraid, alone, and very angry.

The viewing of pornography by one spouse does great damage to marriages. A wife is, at the very least, uncomfortable with her husband looking at other women for the purpose of sexual pleasure. It is not because she is conservative, overly emotional, protective, or jealous. It is because viewing the body of another woman (or man) to pleasure one's self is a violation of the emotional and spiritual bond that connects a husband and a wife, and violation of God's intention for humankind and marriage.

Pornography becomes a competing attachment. And competing attachments hurt. They trigger danger in the attachment system, and for good reason. God intended it to be that way. The couple is alerted that an intruder has entered their sacred bed. And intruders are not supposed to be allowed into the bond between a husband and a wife.

For a woman, pornography is a slap in the face and a stab in the heart. It says to her that she is not good enough, not worthy enough, and not attractive enough to be the source of her spouse's full sexual attention. He has to supplement his needs with other women. She is insufficient. A man may not think of pornography this way, but it is important for him to understand that this is how it affects his wife, and so his marriage.

Men's sexual energy builds and the need to release the energy grows. Since men are visually stimulated, pornography, or watching other women, is very powerful for them. The sight of cleavage peeking out of a low-cut blouse can be very arousing. The man who looks at it has not thought of the woman as a person; he just looks at her cleavage and his body responds. He may think it is innocent enough. But it is not. It is a violation of the woman he gazes at, as well as a violation of his own marriage.

It is of vital importance for men to find a way to share with their wives their attraction to pornography. Wives can serve their husbands as gatekeepers to the marital bed. When a woman understands that a man's sexual drive and ability to be visually stimulated by other women is not a reflection of her inadequacies, but rather of his biological makeup and a powerfully destructive addiction cycle, she can become a great accountability support.

Yes, wives, it is very hurtful to discover that the sight of another woman turns on your husband. Women have a hard time understanding how another woman's body can have so much power over men. Typically, the sight of a well-formed male physique does not arouse women. It would take more than that—a whole lot more. Arousing a woman usually includes romance, caressing, a listening ear, and understanding words.

Therefore, if a wife can understand that pornography is not about her inadequacies, but rather about her husband's biological makeup, then she will be willing to come to the table to talk. At the discussion table, together they can share the impact of the pornography on each of their lives. The husband might admit to the powerful draw he has to pornography, maybe share when he first saw pornography and how it has influenced his life over the years. He can also share about the shame and guilt he has lived with regarding the secrecy of his pornography, and how it leaves him feeling far from all that God has for him. With his wife listening to understand—not to criticize, judge, or punish, but to *understand*—he can also express his desire to switch his sexual focus and energy toward his wife. He can elicit his wife's help in doing so. Together they can go before God for strength in purifying their relationship.

It takes courage for a wife to enter this seemingly "dark side" of her husband's sexuality. It seems scary, evil, foreign, out of control, and so far from where she is. Talking honestly, and not judgmentally, she can share how she fears that his pornography will turn his attention away from her. That she will be thought of less and will endlessly fail at fulfilling his desires or expectations. That she will always fall short of his fantasy and his fantasy women.

A wife can explain how hurt she is every time her husband invites the images of those women into the bed that was intended only for the two of them. She can share her longing to be the center of his desire. Her fear is that, once caught in the hand of pornography, her husband will be closed off to the voice of God in his life. And the fear is that she then will be left alone, without protection, her life in the hands of a godless man.

Once a couple can talk openly together, their fears, hurts, and hopes can be shared. The dragon of pornography can be fought together, rather than the battle being fought between the two of them. It needn't be something that forms a wedge between them, but a dangerous habit that needs to be dealt with *together*.

Most men long to have their wives as the focus of their sexual attention. Once a man can move past his shame, defensiveness, pride, and fears and communicate with his wife, he can move toward building a closer bond with her. And if a woman can get past her own shock, anger, disgust, and pain, she can become a powerful resource to purifying the marital bed.

One husband would call his wife when he was tempted at the office. He recalls, "I was at the office and in walked one of the new reps. She bent over, and her skirt was so short, she revealed everything. I had just told my wife the weekend before that I wanted to include her more in my sexuality. And here I was, very aroused. At lunchtime I felt a strong urge to close my office door and scan a few porn sites. Then I remembered my wife's promise: 'If you call me, I will promise to support you, not criticize you. But please, don't let me find out on my own. That is too hurtful.'

"So I took the risk and called her. She was so understanding, she even thanked me for calling to tell her. She said that it helped build her trust in me when I did this. I started thinking of her body and how sweet our times of lovemaking can be. I kept thinking about how I wanted my wife and not other women. My heart softened and I felt close to my wife. There is no way I could betray her trust after that!"

A SAD STATE OF AFFAIRS

The topic of affairs and how they impact the attachment bond and destroy safe haven marriages is a vast one and probably needs a book all to itself. For now, to show how damaging affairs can be, we will describe one couple, and we will offer some key issues to consider.

Christina thought her husband, Philip, would never betray her. No matter what happened between them, she felt deep inside that they would always be able to work things out. They had already spent many years together and had shared many memories: bringing up children, buying a home, vacations, illnesses, Philip's change of jobs, even raising three puppies. They would be together for their whole lives. She never imagined life without him, even though they argued a lot and had been emotionally disconnected for a while. Still, they would always work it out. They would one day come together and untangle their web of fighting, disagreements, and disconnection.

Then Christina found out. She began to take note of the phone numbers on Philip's cellular phone, the credit card bills, the unexplained late nights, and finally the receipt for a dozen roses she never received. Suddenly it all added up. Her world was shattered. Her heart broke into a thousand pieces. Could this really be happening to her? To her marriage? Not Philip! "How could he do this to me?" she cried. "Doesn't our marriage mean anything to him?"

Every unfaithful man and woman I have counseled has expressed deep regret for having an affair. They admit that the affair tore their family and their lives apart. And they vow that what they really wanted all along was to be connected with their spouse. In fact, most spouses who have had affairs admit that they never actually wanted to leave their wife or husband. Nor was it really about sex.

What we hear, again and again, is that they were longing for, searching for, reaching for a close attachment bond. They yearned to be accepted by and connected to their spouse. But all the fighting and unresolved hurts between them made it seem impossible. As one man said, "I longed to be connected with a woman who loved me no matter what. I innocently started a friendship with my coworker, but then it developed into something more. I really just wanted to be connected to my wife. I didn't want all this chaos and heartache."

One man admitted that his affair happened because his wife told him that she felt he was nothing more than a brother to her. "It broke something in me. I longed to be her hero. I so wanted her to love me. I met the secretary at my friend's office. I was hurting and vulnerable, and she seemed to fill my need. I really didn't want *her* attention. I wanted my wife's admiration and love. But I didn't know how to get it."

Another man admitted, "I loved my wife, but every night we fought. And we fought about every little thing. I was so beaten down. The affair helped me tolerate the chaos at home. Today, I just want to heal our hurts and be close again."

Now let us make one thing clear: *Nothing justifies an affair.* No matter how you slice it, and no matter from which angle you look at it (ask anyone who has had an affair), affairs are devastating and never solve anything. Like pornography, affairs are destructive to your marriage, your life, and the best that God has for you. But affairs sometimes seem to be a path that husbands or wives take in their search to find a safe haven with their spouse. And what a destructive path it is!

Like pornography, an affair is devastating to a marriage because it stabs the attachment bond that connects a husband and a wife. Although the marriage may have been troubled, with the partners unable to enjoy one another, deep down most spouses feel that they will always work things out in the end.

There are many aspects of an affair that devastate a marriage. A husband is torn apart at the thought of his wife being sexually involved with another man. It cuts to his masculinity and the core of his manhood. "I'm not man enough to keep my wife. I am so unworthy as a husband." To mask this sense of failure and pain, a wounded man's hurt and depression are often expressed as anger.

For a woman, the thought of her husband gazing romantically into another woman's eyes and giving her his heart is gut-wrenching. She feels she is not able to draw her husband to herself and keep his attention or interest because she is not good enough. In both cases, wronged spouses admit that their partner's affairs made them feel unworthy, not good enough, less of a man, or unattractive as a woman.

The bottom line is that someone else has been invited into the union that God intended to be solely between the husband and the wife. Affairs, as competing attachments, tug and pull at the heart and cause it to turn from its intended focus: one's spouse.

HEALING AFTER AN AFFAIR

It is not possible to effectively undo the hurt of an affair through a self-help book. Affairs need professional help. The seriousness of an affair is such that often an intermediary is necessary to facilitate healing. Our purpose here has been mainly to identify the pain of affairs, to warn couples of the damaging effects of affairs, and to give comfort and hope. There are a few pointers we can offer, however, that can point you in the direction of healing.

When your spouse has an affair, you lose predictability and trustworthiness. Your spouse is no longer the loved one you once trusted to be there for you. He has become capricious and unfamiliar. For those spouses whose partners have had an affair, it is important to understand why it "made sense" for your partner to have had the affair. What was going on in her mind? Will the affair be repeated? Or will your spouse be able to resolve his hurts and emptiness in healthier ways?

All spouses whose partners have had an affair long to know that their spouse really does love them, does care for them, does choose them, won't do it again, and will from now on have their best interest at heart. They need to understand how they can change the things that made the affair an option. In this way the spouse becomes predictable and safe again. The lover in their bed, who became a stranger when they had the affair, becomes familiar once more.

If you have had an affair and have chosen to stay with your spouse, understand that it will take time for your spouse to heal and for trust to return. Before the affair, your marriage was probably on thin ice, and you may have had a strong pursue-withdraw cycle that left you emotionally disconnected. You may want to keep your marriage, but even so, you do not want to return to the old ways of interacting.

In light of this, healing an affair will consist of the following:

- Pick up the broken hearts and heal the hurt from the affair. You begin by listening to your spouse express his hurt and sorrow, and respond in a caring and compassionate manner.
- Come to terms with the fact that you had the affair, and make sense of why you allowed yourself to do it. Grieve the loss and pain as a result of the affair.
- Heal past relationship hurts that occurred before the affair.
- Undo past hurtful and disconnecting interactional patterns.
- Relearn new ways of interacting.

Healing from an affair also requires juggling such mixed emotions as:

"I love you, and I want to work things out."

"I hate you. How could you have done this to me?"

"I don't want to go back and do things like we did before, but I love you."

"I am hurting. That is one of the reasons why I had the affair, and I need healing myself."

"Don't ever, ever do this to me again, or you will destroy me!"

"I want to forgive you and reconnect our hearts, but I hurt and am angry at you."

In the final analysis, the one who has wandered away just has to accept that it will take time for trust to return. You will have to earn your partner's trust all over again.

Finally, although it is important to take the hurt very seriously, don't make an affair into a catastrophe. It is *not* the end of your marriage—nor of the world. As devastating as it is when you first find out what has happened, just be assured that one year from now, it is possible for you and your spouse to have set a new course in your marriage.

What are the hurts that linger in your marriage? Are they misunderstandings that have been replayed so many times that they have turned into attachment injuries? Do your worst hurts have to do with pornography? Has there been an affair? More than one? Be careful as you face your hurts—whatever the problem, continual angry reactions can compound the already painful impact of the wound and may lead to worse things.

With the help of God, by forgiving and then moving beyond forgiveness into healing and reconnecting, you can successfully build a safe haven marriage. He is willing and able to heal the brokenhearted, to reweave the frayed relationship bonds, and to teach the heartbreaker new ways of living. With Him, all things are possible.

REFLECTION QUESTIONS

1. Have you or your spouse ever experienced an attachment injury? When have you felt that your spouse was not there for you when you needed him or her? What happened?

2. How has your relationship been affected by this injury?

3. Have you forgiven your spouse? At this time, what prevents you from taking the risk to open your heart to your spouse and walk along the path of emotionally reconnecting?

4. What are some ways that you and your spouse can rebuild trust?

5. How can you protect your relationship from temptations and unhealed wounds?

CASE STUDY AND OVERVIEW OF FOSTERING A SAFE HAVEN MARRIAGE

*T*o pull this all together, we share the experience of Scott and Carin. They have walked all the way through the process of turning their emotionally disconnected relationship into a safe haven marriage. It has not been easy, as it has required each of them to become vulnerable and to risk putting their hearts into each other's hands. But the blessings that have followed have been bountiful. They now have a safe place where they know they are loved, seen, and accepted. They can count on each other to be trustworthy, emotionally available, and responsive. They are each other's haven of safety. Let's review their experience:

THE ATTACHMENT STYLE BROUGHT TO THE RELATIONSHIP

There are four attachment styles: secure, anxious, avoidant, and fearful. Our attachment style determines how we regulate our emotions and view ourselves, others, and the world around us.

Carin has a more anxious attachment style: Carin fears that Scott will not love her as much as she loves him. She has always feared that he will find her a disappointment and not value her. Whenever she senses that Scott is emotionally inaccessible or doesn't acknowledge her feelings, she feels hurt and angry.

Scott has a more avoidant attachment style and is guarded and feels that it is best to be self-sufficient and independent, although he longs to be close and loved by Carin. He often doesn't know what to do with Carin's emotions and needs and then feels attacked, so he avoids her emotions and protects himself.

THE INTERACTIONAL CYCLE

When our attachment bond is threatened, or we sense that our spouse is emotionally unavailable or unresponsive, we react in an attempt to protest the disconnection, protect our heart, and pull from our spouse a caring response.

The four options of responding when we feel unseen, unloved, misunderstood, or rejected are: pursue, withdraw, freeze, or tend and care.

Carin tends to pursue. She explains: "You say something that hurts me, and I try to tell you how hurt I am."

Scott tends to withdraw. He explains: "I listen to you and try to explain what I mean because you are unfairly attacking me."

"I hear you defending yourself and not understanding how I feel, so I shout louder and tell you that you are wrong."

"You raise your voice, and my defenses go up. You talk down to me. I can't phrase things as well as you. I feel misunderstood and frustrated."

"I tell you that you don't understand. I use an intense tone of voice because you don't see how you've hurt me. I tell you how wrong you are."

"At this point I feel there's nothing I can do to change your image of me. I can't be compassionate, so I shut down and withdraw."

"I sense that you have shut down. I feel desperate and angry."

"I feel I have to leave until things have cooled down. Our argument isn't going anywhere, so I step back."

"THORN" EMOTIONS THAT FUEL THE CYCLE

These are the emotions and behaviors that are expressed to your spouse when you feel hurt. You express these emotions when it is too difficult to share your inner heart. These emotions help protect your softer side and can cloud all you feel. They fuel your negative ways of relating.

THE THORNS	
Pursuer's Secondary Emotional Experience	*Withdrawer's Secondary Emotional Experience*
Angry, frustrated, resentful, hurt (mixed with anger)	Frustrated, hurt, disappointed, helpless
RESPOND BY	
Going after, attacking, blaming, criticizing, pointing out wrongs, heightening emotions	Avoiding, self-protection, de-escalating conflict, distancing, hiding away, walking on eggshells, cautious, staying away from emotions
Carin's experience: "I get angry, yell, accuse him of being aloof, thoughtless, and not caring about me. I criticize him and we fight. Then I go into my room, slam the door (that is my way of letting him know I am hurt), and cry."	Scott's experience: "I feel frustrated that she sees me this way, that there's nothing I can do to make her not believe this about me. I defend myself, but when it doesn't make a difference, I withdraw, I get busy, I shut her out."

ROOT OR PRIMARY EMOTIONS

Under the harsh, secondary emotions are often tender, softer emotions. It is what you are feeling as you are criticizing or withdrawing. These emotions, when expressed honestly, can fuel more open and honest ways of relating.

THE ROOTS

Pursuer's Primary Emotional Experience	Withdrawer's Primary Emotional Experience
Fear of rejection, abandonment, lonely, tired, worthless, unlovable	Fear of being inadequate, overwhelmed, alone, not good enough, failure, shame
(Women usually identify feelings associated with lack of connection and deprivation of contact.)	(Men identify feelings of inadequacy and incompetence.)
Carin's softer emotions: "I feel afraid, lonely, rejected, left alone, abandoned, far away from him."	Scott's softer emotions: "No matter what I do, it's not good enough. I will always fall short. It's sad. I feel frustrated and lose hope."

DISCOVERING THE LONGINGS OF THE HEART

Pursuer's Heart Longings and Needs	Withdrawer's Heart Longings and Needs
To be loved, accepted, understood, and valued, to belong, to be pursued, to be found worthy	Affirmation, trust, confidence, companionship, accepted, respected.
Carin's longings: "I long for him to tell me that he values me, to sit and	Scott's longings: "I long for her to affirm me and see my value as her

listen to me, and to understand how I feel. I want him to tell me that he chooses me and loves me. I want him to reach through my porcupine quills and pull me close."

husband and respect me. I long for her to trust me, accept me, and be a companion to me."

SHARING YOUR HEART, NEEDS, AND LONGINGS

As you and your spouse are able to share your feelings and needs from a less critical position, or instead of withdrawing, you are able to build empathy and understanding for each other, be there for each other, and emotionally connect.

Carin says: "I never knew you felt so hurt by my attacks. I want you to feel valued and respected. I just need you to stay connected and not pull away."

Scott says: "I never knew you were scared of being alone. I don't want you to hurt. I just can't come close to you when you are attacking me."

"I want you to understand that under my harsh words, criticism, and pursuing is a longing for you to pull me close to your heart and love me. I need you to try to understand me and work as a team."

"I am not the perfect spouse. I will grow and try to be more engaged, but I need you to accept me, value me, and then grow with me as we learn to be there for each other."

As you build understanding, empathy, acceptance and are willing to change,

A NEW CYCLE BEGINS

Carin shares: "Yes, I know that in the past I have come at you with my thorns and criticism. And I know that you may be very apprehensive

Scott shares: "Yes, I know I have let you down in the past. I have not been there. I have shut you out and hurt you. I know it will be a risk for as to whether the changes will last. But be honest and come alongside me if I get critical. I will try reaching for you from my heart instead of with my thorns. I don't want to hurt you like I have in the past. You are my prince and I value you."

you to trust that I will value your feelings and team with you. I ask that you help me in this process, together we can learn how to be there for each other. You are my princess and I cherish you."

Appendix B

ADDITIONAL READING
RESOURCES

Ainsworth, M., M. Blhar, El Waters, and S. Wall. *Patterns of Attachment.* Hillsdale, N.J.: Erlbaum, 1978.*

Arp, D., and C. Arp. *10 Great Dates to Energize Your Marriage.* Grand Rapids, Mich.: Zondervan, 1997.

Bartholomew, K., and L. Horowitz. "Attachment Styles among Young Adults: A Test of a Four Category Model." *Journal of Personality and Social Psychology* 61 (1991): 226–44.*

Bowlby, J. *Attachment and Loss.* Vol. 1. New York: Basic, 1969.

Bowlby, J. *A Secure Base.* New York: Basic, 1988.

Bowlby, J. *The Making and Breaking of Affectional Bonds.* London: Routledge, 1979.

Cassidy, J., and P. Shaver. *Handbook of Attachment*. New York: Guilford, 1999.*

Christensen, A., and N. S. Jacobson. *Reconcilable Differences*. New York: Guildford, 2000.

Faber, A., and E. Mazlish. *How to Talk So Kids Will Listen and Listen So Kids Will Talk*. New York: Avon, 1980.

Hart, A. D. *The Sexual Man: Masculinity without Guilt*. Nashville: Word, 1994.

Hart, A.D., C H. Hart Weber, and D. L. Taylor. *Secrets of Eve: Understanding the Mystery of Female Sexuality*. Nashville: Word, 1998.

Hart Morris, S. "Creating a Safe and Close Connection." In Stoop, D. and J. Stoop. *The Complete Marriage Book*. Grand Rapids, Mich.: Revell, 2002.

Hart Morris, S. "Emotionally Focused Couples Therapy." *Marriage and Family: A Christian Journal* 5 (2002): 145–55.*

Hart Morris, S. "Love, Sex, and Marriage: Working Out Our Most Intimate Relationship." In Clinton, T., and G. Sibcy, *Attachments*. Brentwood, Tenn.: Integrity, 2002.

Hazan, C., and P. Shaver. "Romantic Love Conceptualized As an Attachment Process." *Journal of Personality and Social Psychology* 52 (1987): 511–24.*

Johnson, S. M. "Bonds and Bargains: Relationship Paradigms and Their Significance for Marital Therapy." *Journal of Marital and Family Therapy* 12 (1986): 259–67.*

Johnson, S. M. *The Practice of Emotionally Focused Marital Therapy: Creating Connection*. New York: Brunner/Mazel, 1996.*

Johnson, S. M., and L. S. Greenberg, eds. *The Heart of the Matter: Perspectives on Emotion in Marital Therapy.* New York: Brunner/Mazel, 1994.*

Johnson, S. M., and L. S. Greenberg. *Emotionally Focused Therapy for Couples.* New York: Guilford, 1988.*

Johnson, S. M, J. A. Makinen, and J. W. Millikin. "Attachment Injuries in Couple Relationships: A New Perspective on Impasses in Couples Therapy." *Journal of Marital and Family Therapy* 27, no. 2 (April 2001): 145–55.*

Markman, H., S. Stanley, and S. L. Blumberg. *Fighting for Your Marriage.* Jossey-Bass: San Ellenco, 1994.

Simpson, J. A., W. S. Rholes, and J. S. Nelligan. "Support Seeking and Support Giving within Couples in an Anxiety-Provoking Situation: The Role of Attachment Styles." *Journal of Personality and Social Psychology* 62 (1992): 434–46.*

Simpson, J. A., W. S. Rholes, and D. Phillips. "Conflict in Close Relationships: An Attachment Perspective." *Journal of Personality and Social Psychology* 71, no. 5 (November 1996): 899–914.*

* Denotes books and journal articles that are academically focused or geared for counselors.

Appendix C

MORE INFORMATION ON SAFE HAVEN MARRIAGES, EMOTIONALLY FOCUSED THERAPY, AND SAFE HAVEN PARENTING

Workshops

For information on safe haven marriage and safe haven parenting workshops, retreats, couples' seminars, or further training in emotionally focused therapy for pastors or counselors, please write or e-mail us.

Marital Scale

To order the complete Haven of Safety Scale, please obtain information on how to do so by going to our Web site, www.havenofsafety.com, or write or e-mail us.

Other Materials

To obtain a copy of the upcoming video series, couple's daily inspirational calendar, and couple's workbook, write to us or visit our Web site. You may also request a list of Dr. Archibald Hart's books and audiotapes.

Haven of Safety
c/o Dr. Sharon Hart Morris
1042 Cyrus Lane
Arcadia, CA 91006

sharon@sharonhartmorris.com
www.havenofsafety.com

NOTES

Introduction

1. A. Christensen, and N. S. Jacobson, *Reconcilable Differences* (New York: Guilford, 2000), xiv.

Chapter 3: Is Your Marriage a Safe Haven?

1. The Haven of Safety Scale (© June 12, 2000) is offered here for your personal use only. You are not authorized to copy the test for anyone but yourself. If you are a counselor and wish to use the test in couples' counseling, you may obtain copies of the complete scale in booklet form that outlines it in more detail, including details of how to score and interpret the scale, and how to use the scale in counseling. (See Appendix C.)

Chapter 5: How Do Your Hearts Connect?

1. C. Hazan, and P. Shaver, "Romantic Love Conceptualized As an Attachment

Process." *Journal of Personality and Social Psychology* 52 (1987): 511–24.

2. K. Bartholomew, and L. Horowitz, "Attachment Styles among Young Adults: A Test of a Four Category Model." *Journal of Personality and Social Psychology* 61 (1991): 226–44.

3. Adapted from ibid.

4. J. A. Simpson, W. S. Rholes, and D. Phillips, "Conflict in Close Relationships: An Attachment Perspective," *Journal of Personality and Social Psychology* 71, no. 5 (November 1996): 899–914.

5. This attachment style questionnaire is adapted from Bartholomew and Horowitz, "Attachment Styles among Young Adults."

Chapter 6: Patterns That Leave Couples Emotionally Disconnected
1. Adapted from research conducted by Don Peterson of Rutgers University.

Chapter 8: Emotionally Reconnecting
1. The withdrawer engaging and the pursuer softening steps are adapted from the nine steps of bringing about change in couples, found in S. Johnson and L. Greenberg's *Emotionally Focused Therapy for Couples* (New York: Guilford Press, 1988), and S. Johnson, *Creating Connections* (New York: Brunner/Mazel, 1996).

Chapter 9: Healing Hurts of the Heart
1. The steps of healing attachment injuries are adapted from the steps of healing found in S. M. Johnson, J. A. Makinen, and J. W. Millikin, "Attachment Injuries in Couple Relationships: A New Perspective on Impasses in Couples Therapy," *Journal of Marital and Family Therapy* 27, no. 2 (April 2001): 145–55.

ABOUT THE AUTHORS

Archibald Daniel Hart, Ph.D., FPPR, is Professor of Psychology and Dean Emeritus of Fuller Graduate School of Psychology, Fuller Theological Seminary, Pasadena, California. He also serves as the Executive Editor and Director of International Relations for the American Association of Christian Counselors. He is an internationally known speaker and author, whose books include *Adrenaline and Stress, Children and Divorce, The Sexual Man, The Anxiety Cure,* and many others.

Sharon Hart Morris, Ph.D., is the cofounder and Director of the Marriage, Family, and Relationship Institute at La Vie Counseling Center in Pasadena, California. She received her Ph.D. in marriage and family therapy from Fuller Graduate School of Psychology and is a licensed marriage and family therapist. She is the author of numerous articles and chapters in books on relationships and an expert in emotionally focused therapy. She is a contributing editor for *Marriage and Family: A Christian Journal.* Dr. Morris teaches internationally and contributes regularly to both broadcast and print media.

LaVergne, TN USA
26 July 2010
190892LV00011B/8/A